The Tragedie of
Macbeth

By Edward de Vere

Art:
Portrait of Edward de Vere
17th Earl of Oxford (1550-1604)

This edition produced by
Verus Publishing

V | P

www.verusbooks.com

ISBN: 978-1-951267-31-5
Imprint / Publisher: Verus Publishing

The Author

Edward de Vere, 17th Earl of Oxford

Biography and Bibliography
After the Play

A Preverse

Drone on ye learned scholars of the day
As to with whom the words ahead the credit lay.
For our part though can be no further doubt
That the author of these words has been found out
To be a person lordly and refined
On whom the light of wit so boldly shined
That to keep this wit from tearing in the fray
He gave another, lesser wit his say.

Now let the least of wits
That writes these paltry lines
Yield to him whose peerless name
Should be with reverence spake.
Let this name be not of history's misassigns
Whose pen and verse have made the earth to shake.

The Tragedie of
Macbeth

By Edward de Vere

The Main Characters

Duncan - King of Scotland.

Malcolm - Elder son of Duncan

Donalbain - Younder son of Duncan

Macbeth - A general in the army of Duncan.

Lady Macbeth - Macbeth's wife.

Banquo - Macbeth's friend and fellow general.

Fleance - Son of Banquo.

Macduff - The Thane of Fife.

Lady Macduff - Macduff's wife.

Macduff's Son

Ross, Lennox, Angus, Menteith, Caithness -
    Noblemen of Scotland

Siward - English general.

Hecate - Queen of the Witches.

Three Witches

Three Murderers

Doctor -Lady Macbeth's doctor.

And now, the Play...

ACT I

SCENE I.

A desert place.

Thunder and lightning. Enter three Witches

First Witch
    When shall we three meet again
    In thunder, lightning, or in rain?
Second Witch
    When the hurlyburly's done,
    When the battle's lost and won.
Third Witch
    That will be ere the set of sun.
First Witch
    Where the place?
Second Witch
    Upon the heath.
Third Witch
    There to meet with Macbeth.
First Witch
    I come, Graymalkin!
Second Witch
    Paddock calls.
Third Witch
    Anon.
ALL
    Fair is foul, and foul is fair:
    Hover through the fog and filthy air.

Exeunt

SCENE II.

A camp near Forres.

Alarum within. Enter DUNCAN, MALCOLM, DONALBAIN, LENNOX, with Attendants, meeting a bleeding Sergeant

DUNCAN
>What bloody man is that? He can report,
>As seemeth by his plight, of the revolt
>The newest state.

MALCOLM
>This is the sergeant
>Who like a good and hardy soldier fought
>'Gainst my captivity. Hail, brave friend!
>Say to the king the knowledge of the broil
>As thou didst leave it.

Sergeant
>Doubtful it stood;
>As two spent swimmers, that do cling together
>And choke their art. The merciless Macdonwald--
>Worthy to be a rebel, for to that
>The multiplying villanies of nature
>Do swarm upon him--from the western isles
>Of kerns and gallowglasses is supplied;
>And fortune, on his damned quarrel smiling,
>Show'd like a rebel's whore: but all's too weak:
>For brave Macbeth--well he deserves that name--
>Disdaining fortune, with his brandish'd steel,
>Which smoked with bloody execution,
>Like valour's minion carved out his passage
>Till he faced the slave;
>Which ne'er shook hands, nor bade farewell to him,
>Till he unseam'd him from the nave to the chaps,
>And fix'd his head upon our battlements.

DUNCAN

O valiant cousin! worthy gentleman!

Sergeant

As whence the sun 'gins his reflection
Shipwrecking storms and direful thunders break,
So from that spring whence comfort seem'd to come
Discomfort swells. Mark, king of Scotland, mark:
No sooner justice had with valour arm'd
Compell'd these skipping kerns to trust their heels,
But the Norweyan lord surveying vantage,
With furbish'd arms and new supplies of men
Began a fresh assault.

DUNCAN

Dismay'd not this
Our captains, Macbeth and Banquo?

Sergeant

Yes;
As sparrows eagles, or the hare the lion.
If I say sooth, I must report they were
As cannons overcharged with double cracks, so they
Doubly redoubled strokes upon the foe:
Except they meant to bathe in reeking wounds,
Or memorise another Golgotha,
I cannot tell.
But I am faint, my gashes cry for help.

DUNCAN

So well thy words become thee as thy wounds;
They smack of honour both. Go get him surgeons.

Exit Sergeant, attended

Who comes here?

Enter ROSS

MALCOLM

The worthy thane of Ross.

LENNOX

> What a haste looks through his eyes! So should he look
> That seems to speak things strange.

ROSS

> God save the king!

DUNCAN

> Whence camest thou, worthy thane?

ROSS

> From Fife, great king;
> Where the Norweyan banners flout the sky
> And fan our people cold. Norway himself,
> With terrible numbers,
> Assisted by that most disloyal traitor
> The thane of Cawdor, began a dismal conflict;
> Till that Bellona's bridegroom, lapp'd in proof,
> Confronted him with self-comparisons,
> Point against point rebellious, arm 'gainst arm.
> Curbing his lavish spirit: and, to conclude,
> The victory fell on us.

DUNCAN

> Great happiness!

ROSS

> That now
> Sweno, the Norways' king, craves composition:
> Nor would we deign him burial of his men
> Till he disbursed at Saint Colme's inch
> Ten thousand dollars to our general use.

DUNCAN

> No more that thane of Cawdor shall deceive
> Our bosom interest: go pronounce his present death,
> And with his former title greet Macbeth.

ROSS

> I'll see it done.

DUNCAN
What he hath lost noble Macbeth hath won.

Exeunt

SCENE III.

A heath near Forres.

Thunder. Enter the three Witches

First Witch
Where hast thou been, sister?
Second Witch
Killing swine.
Third Witch
Sister, where thou?
First Witch
A sailor's wife had chestnuts in her lap,
And munch'd, and munch'd, and munch'd:--
'Give me,' quoth I:
'Aroint thee, witch!' the rump-fed ronyon cries.
Her husband's to Aleppo gone, master o' the Tiger:
But in a sieve I'll thither sail,
And, like a rat without a tail,
I'll do, I'll do, and I'll do.
Second Witch
I'll give thee a wind.
First Witch
Thou'rt kind.
Third Witch
And I another.
First Witch
I myself have all the other,
And the very ports they blow,
All the quarters that they know

I' the shipman's card.
I will drain him dry as hay:
Sleep shall neither night nor day
Hang upon his pent-house lid;
' He shall live a man forbid:
Weary se'nnights nine times nine
Shall he dwindle, peak and pine:
Though his bark cannot be lost,
Yet it shall be tempest-tost.
Look what I have.
Second Witch
Show me, show me.
First Witch
Here I have a pilot's thumb,
Wreck'd as homeward he did come.

Drum within

Third Witch
A drum, a drum!
Macbeth doth come.
ALL
The weird sisters, hand in hand,
Posters of the sea and land,
Thus do go about, about:
Thrice to thine and thrice to mine
And thrice again, to make up nine.
Peace! the charm's wound up.

Enter MACBETH and BANQUO

MACBETH
So foul and fair a day I have not seen.
BANQUO
How far is't call'd to Forres? What are these

So wither'd and so wild in their attire,
That look not like the inhabitants o' the earth,
And yet are on't? Live you? or are you aught
That man may question? You seem to understand me,
By each at once her chappy finger laying
Upon her skinny lips: you should be women,
And yet your beards forbid me to interpret
That you are so.
MACBETH
Speak, if you can: what are you?
First Witch
All hail, Macbeth! hail to thee, thane of Glamis!
Second Witch
All hail, Macbeth, hail to thee, thane of Cawdor!
Third Witch
All hail, Macbeth, thou shalt be king hereafter!
BANQUO
Good sir, why do you start; and seem to fear
Things that do sound so fair? I' the name of truth,
Are ye fantastical, or that indeed
Which outwardly ye show? My noble partner
You greet with present grace and great prediction
Of noble having and of royal hope,
That he seems rapt withal: to me you speak not.
If you can look into the seeds of time,
And say which grain will grow and which will not,
Speak then to me, who neither beg nor fear
Your favours nor your hate.
First Witch
Hail!
Second Witch
Hail!
Third Witch
Hail!

First Witch
    Lesser than Macbeth, and greater.
Second Witch
    Not so happy, yet much happier.
Third Witch
    Thou shalt get kings, though thou be none:
    So all hail, Macbeth and Banquo!
First Witch
    Banquo and Macbeth, all hail!
MACBETH
    Stay, you imperfect speakers, tell me more:
    By Sinel's death I know I am thane of Glamis;
    But how of Cawdor? the thane of Cawdor lives,
    A prosperous gentleman; and to be king
    Stands not within the prospect of belief,
    No more than to be Cawdor. Say from whence
    You owe this strange intelligence? or why
    Upon this blasted heath you stop our way
    With such prophetic greeting? Speak, I charge you.

Witches vanish

BANQUO
    The earth hath bubbles, as the water has,
    And these are of them. Whither are they vanish'd?
MACBETH
    Into the air; and what seem'd corporal melted
    As breath into the wind. Would they had stay'd!
BANQUO
    Were such things here as we do speak about?
    Or have we eaten on the insane root
    That takes the reason prisoner?
MACBETH
    Your children shall be kings.
BANQUO

You shall be king.

MACBETH

And thane of Cawdor too: went it not so?

BANQUO

To the selfsame tune and words. Who's here?

Enter ROSS and ANGUS

ROSS

The king hath happily received, Macbeth,
The news of thy success; and when he reads
Thy personal venture in the rebels' fight,
His wonders and his praises do contend
Which should be thine or his: silenced with that,
In viewing o'er the rest o' the selfsame day,
He finds thee in the stout Norweyan ranks,
Nothing afeard of what thyself didst make,
Strange images of death. As thick as hail
Came post with post; and every one did bear
Thy praises in his kingdom's great defence,
And pour'd them down before him.

ANGUS

We are sent
To give thee from our royal master thanks;
Only to herald thee into his sight,
Not pay thee.

ROSS

And, for an earnest of a greater honour,
He bade me, from him, call thee thane of Cawdor:
In which addition, hail, most worthy thane!
For it is thine.

BANQUO

What, can the devil speak true?

MACBETH

The thane of Cawdor lives: why do you dress me

In borrow'd robes?
ANGUS
Who was the thane lives yet;
But under heavy judgment bears that life
Which he deserves to lose. Whether he was combined
With those of Norway, or did line the rebel
With hidden help and vantage, or that with both
He labour'd in his country's wreck, I know not;
But treasons capital, confess'd and proved,
Have overthrown him.
MACBETH
[Aside] Glamis, and thane of Cawdor!
The greatest is behind.

To ROSS and ANGUS

Thanks for your pains.

To BANQUO

Do you not hope your children shall be kings,
When those that gave the thane of Cawdor to me
Promised no less to them?
BANQUO
That trusted home
Might yet enkindle you unto the crown,
Besides the thane of Cawdor. But 'tis strange:
And oftentimes, to win us to our harm,
The instruments of darkness tell us truths,
Win us with honest trifles, to betray's
In deepest consequence.
Cousins, a word, I pray you.
MACBETH
[Aside]   Two truths are told,
As happy prologues to the swelling act

Of the imperial theme.--I thank you, gentlemen.

Aside

Cannot be ill, cannot be good: if ill,
Why hath it given me earnest of success,
Commencing in a truth? I am thane of Cawdor:
If good, why do I yield to that suggestion
Whose horrid image doth unfix my hair
And make my seated heart knock at my ribs,
Against the use of nature? Present fears
Are less than horrible imaginings:
My thought, whose murder yet is but fantastical,
Shakes so my single state of man that function
Is smother'd in surmise, and nothing is
But what is not.
BANQUO
Look, how our partner's rapt.
MACBETH
[Aside] If chance will have me king, why, chance may
crown me,
Without my stir.
BANQUO
New horrors come upon him,
Like our strange garments, cleave not to their mould
But with the aid of use.
MACBETH
[Aside] Come what come may,
Time and the hour runs through the roughest day.
BANQUO
Worthy Macbeth, we stay upon your leisure.
MACBETH
Give me your favour: my dull brain was wrought
With things forgotten. Kind gentlemen, your pains
Are register'd where every day I turn

The leaf to read them. Let us toward the king.
Think upon what hath chanced, and, at more time,
The interim having weigh'd it, let us speak
Our free hearts each to other.
BANQUO
    Very gladly.
MACBETH
    Till then, enough. Come, friends.

Exeunt

SCENE IV.

Forres. The palace.

*Flourish. Enter DUNCAN, MALCOLM, DONALBAIN,
LENNOX, and Attendants*

DUNCAN
    Is execution done on Cawdor? Are not
    Those in commission yet return'd?
MALCOLM
    My liege,
    They are not yet come back. But I have spoke
    With one that saw him die: who did report
    That very frankly he confess'd his treasons,
    Implored your highness' pardon and set forth
    A deep repentance: nothing in his life
    Became him like the leaving it; he died
    As one that had been studied in his death
    To throw away the dearest thing he owed,
    As 'twere a careless trifle.
DUNCAN
    There's no art
    To find the mind's construction in the face:
    He was a gentleman on whom I built

An absolute trust.

Enter MACBETH, BANQUO, ROSS, and ANGUS

O worthiest cousin!
The sin of my ingratitude even now
Was heavy on me: thou art so far before
That swiftest wing of recompense is slow
To overtake thee. Would thou hadst less deserved,
That the proportion both of thanks and payment
Might have been mine! only I have left to say,
More is thy due than more than all can pay.
MACBETH
The service and the loyalty I owe,
In doing it, pays itself. Your highness' part
Is to receive our duties; and our duties
Are to your throne and state children and servants,
Which do but what they should, by doing every thing
Safe toward your love and honour.
DUNCAN
Welcome hither:
I have begun to plant thee, and will labour
To make thee full of growing. Noble Banquo,
That hast no less deserved, nor must be known
No less to have done so, let me enfold thee
And hold thee to my heart.
BANQUO
There if I grow,
The harvest is your own.
DUNCAN
My plenteous joys,
Wanton in fulness, seek to hide themselves
In drops of sorrow. Sons, kinsmen, thanes,
And you whose places are the nearest, know
We will establish our estate upon

Our eldest, Malcolm, whom we name hereafter
The Prince of Cumberland; which honour must
Not unaccompanied invest him only,
But signs of nobleness, like stars, shall shine
On all deservers. From hence to Inverness,
And bind us further to you.

MACBETH
The rest is labour, which is not used for you:
I'll be myself the harbinger and make joyful
The hearing of my wife with your approach;
So humbly take my leave.

DUNCAN
My worthy Cawdor!

MACBETH
[Aside] The Prince of Cumberland! that is a step
On which I must fall down, or else o'erleap,
For in my way it lies. Stars, hide your fires;
Let not light see my black and deep desires:
The eye wink at the hand; yet let that be,
Which the eye fears, when it is done, to see.

Exit

DUNCAN
True, worthy Banquo; he is full so valiant,
And in his commendations I am fed;
It is a banquet to me. Let's after him,
Whose care is gone before to bid us welcome:
It is a peerless kinsman.

Flourish. Exeunt

SCENE V.

Inverness. Macbeth's castle.

Enter LADY MACBETH, reading a letter

LADY MACBETH

'They met me in the day of success: and I have
learned by the perfectest report, they have more in
them than mortal knowledge. When I burned in desire
to question them further, they made themselves air,
into which they vanished. Whiles I stood rapt in
the wonder of it, came missives from the king, who
all-hailed me 'Thane of Cawdor;' by which title,
before, these weird sisters saluted me, and referred
me to the coming on of time, with 'Hail, king that
shalt be!' This have I thought good to deliver
thee, my dearest partner of greatness, that thou
mightst not lose the dues of rejoicing, by being
ignorant of what greatness is promised thee. Lay it
to thy heart, and farewell.'
Glamis thou art, and Cawdor; and shalt be
What thou art promised: yet do I fear thy nature;
It is too full o' the milk of human kindness
To catch the nearest way: thou wouldst be great;
Art not without ambition, but without
The illness should attend it: what thou wouldst highly,
That wouldst thou holily; wouldst not play false,
And yet wouldst wrongly win: thou'ldst have, great
Glamis,
That which cries 'Thus thou must do, if thou have it;
And that which rather thou dost fear to do
Than wishest should be undone.' Hie thee hither,
That I may pour my spirits in thine ear;
And chastise with the valour of my tongue
All that impedes thee from the golden round,

Which fate and metaphysical aid doth seem
To have thee crown'd withal.

Enter a Messenger

What is your tidings?
Messenger
 The king comes here to-night.
LADY MACBETH
 Thou'rt mad to say it:
 Is not thy master with him? who, were't so,
 Would have inform'd for preparation.
Messenger
 So please you, it is true: our thane is coming:
 One of my fellows had the speed of him,
 Who, almost dead for breath, had scarcely more
 Than would make up his message.
LADY MACBETH
 Give him tending;
 He brings great news.

Exit Messenger

The raven himself is hoarse
That croaks the fatal entrance of Duncan
Under my battlements. Come, you spirits
That tend on mortal thoughts, unsex me here,
And fill me from the crown to the toe top-full
Of direst cruelty! make thick my blood;
Stop up the access and passage to remorse,
That no compunctious visitings of nature
Shake my fell purpose, nor keep peace between
The effect and it! Come to my woman's breasts,
And take my milk for gall, you murdering ministers,
Wherever in your sightless substances

You wait on nature's mischief! Come, thick night,
And pall thee in the dunnest smoke of hell,
That my keen knife see not the wound it makes,
Nor heaven peep through the blanket of the dark,
To cry 'Hold, hold!'

Enter MACBETH

Great Glamis! worthy Cawdor!
Greater than both, by the all-hail hereafter!
Thy letters have transported me beyond
This ignorant present, and I feel now
The future in the instant.

MACBETH
My dearest love,
Duncan comes here to-night.

LADY MACBETH
And when goes hence?

MACBETH
To-morrow, as he purposes.

LADY MACBETH
O, never
Shall sun that morrow see!
Your face, my thane, is as a book where men
May read strange matters. To beguile the time,
Look like the time; bear welcome in your eye,
Your hand, your tongue: look like the innocent flower,
But be the serpent under't. He that's coming
Must be provided for: and you shall put
This night's great business into my dispatch;
Which shall to all our nights and days to come
Give solely sovereign sway and masterdom.

MACBETH
We will speak further.

LADY MACBETH

Only look up clear;
To alter favour ever is to fear:
Leave all the rest to me.

Exeunt

SCENE VI.

Before Macbeth's castle.

*Hautboys and torches. Enter DUNCAN, MALCOLM,
DONALBAIN, BANQUO, LENNOX, MACDUFF, ROSS,
ANGUS, and Attendants*

DUNCAN
This castle hath a pleasant seat; the air
Nimbly and sweetly recommends itself
Unto our gentle senses.
BANQUO
This guest of summer,
The temple-haunting martlet, does approve,
By his loved mansionry, that the heaven's breath
Smells wooingly here: no jutty, frieze,
Buttress, nor coign of vantage, but this bird
Hath made his pendent bed and procreant cradle:
Where they most breed and haunt, I have observed,
The air is delicate.

Enter LADY MACBETH

DUNCAN
See, see, our honour'd hostess!
The love that follows us sometime is our trouble,
Which still we thank as love. Herein I teach you
How you shall bid God 'ild us for your pains,
And thank us for your trouble.
LADY MACBETH

All our service
In every point twice done and then done double
Were poor and single business to contend
Against those honours deep and broad wherewith
Your majesty loads our house: for those of old,
And the late dignities heap'd up to them,
We rest your hermits.

DUNCAN
Where's the thane of Cawdor?
We coursed him at the heels, and had a purpose
To be his purveyor: but he rides well;
And his great love, sharp as his spur, hath holp him
To his home before us. Fair and noble hostess,
We are your guest to-night.

LADY MACBETH
Your servants ever
Have theirs, themselves and what is theirs, in compt,
To make their audit at your highness' pleasure,
Still to return your own.

DUNCAN
Give me your hand;
Conduct me to mine host: we love him highly,
And shall continue our graces towards him.
By your leave, hostess.

Exeunt

SCENE VII.

Macbeth's castle.

*Hautboys and torches. Enter a Sewer, and divers Servants
with dishes and service, and pass over the stage. Then enter
MACBETH*

MACBETH

If it were done when 'tis done, then 'twere well
It were done quickly: if the assassination
Could trammel up the consequence, and catch
With his surcease success; that but this blow
Might be the be-all and the end-all here,
But here, upon this bank and shoal of time,
We'ld jump the life to come. But in these cases
We still have judgment here; that we but teach
Bloody instructions, which, being taught, return
To plague the inventor: this even-handed justice
Commends the ingredients of our poison'd chalice
To our own lips. He's here in double trust;
First, as I am his kinsman and his subject,
Strong both against the deed; then, as his host,
Who should against his murderer shut the door,
Not bear the knife myself. Besides, this Duncan
Hath borne his faculties so meek, hath been
So clear in his great office, that his virtues
Will plead like angels, trumpet-tongued, against
The deep damnation of his taking-off;
And pity, like a naked new-born babe,
Striding the blast, or heaven's cherubim, horsed
Upon the sightless couriers of the air,
Shall blow the horrid deed in every eye,
That tears shall drown the wind. I have no spur
To prick the sides of my intent, but only
Vaulting ambition, which o'erleaps itself
And falls on the other.

Enter LADY MACBETH

How now! what news?
LADY MACBETH
He has almost supp'd: why have you left the chamber?
MACBETH

Hath he ask'd for me?
LADY MACBETH
Know you not he has?
MACBETH
We will proceed no further in this business:
He hath honour'd me of late; and I have bought
Golden opinions from all sorts of people,
Which would be worn now in their newest gloss,
Not cast aside so soon.
LADY MACBETH
Was the hope drunk
Wherein you dress'd yourself? hath it slept since?
And wakes it now, to look so green and pale
At what it did so freely? From this time
Such I account thy love. Art thou afeard
To be the same in thine own act and valour
As thou art in desire? Wouldst thou have that
Which thou esteem'st the ornament of life,
And live a coward in thine own esteem,
Letting 'I dare not' wait upon 'I would,'
Like the poor cat i' the adage?
MACBETH
Prithee, peace:
I dare do all that may become a man;
Who dares do more is none.
LADY MACBETH
What beast was't, then,
That made you break this enterprise to me?
When you durst do it, then you were a man;
And, to be more than what you were, you would
Be so much more the man. Nor time nor place
Did then adhere, and yet you would make both:
They have made themselves, and that their fitness now
Does unmake you. I have given suck, and know

How tender 'tis to love the babe that milks me:
I would, while it was smiling in my face,
Have pluck'd my nipple from his boneless gums,
And dash'd the brains out, had I so sworn as you
Have done to this.

MACBETH
If we should fail?

LADY MACBETH
We fail!
But screw your courage to the sticking-place,
And we'll not fail. When Duncan is asleep--
Whereto the rather shall his day's hard journey
Soundly invite him--his two chamberlains
Will I with wine and wassail so convince
That memory, the warder of the brain,
Shall be a fume, and the receipt of reason
A limbeck only: when in swinish sleep
Their drenched natures lie as in a death,
What cannot you and I perform upon
The unguarded Duncan? what not put upon
His spongy officers, who shall bear the guilt
Of our great quell?

MACBETH
Bring forth men-children only;
For thy undaunted mettle should compose
Nothing but males. Will it not be received,
When we have mark'd with blood those sleepy two
Of his own chamber and used their very daggers,
That they have done't?

LADY MACBETH
Who dares receive it other,
As we shall make our griefs and clamour roar
Upon his death?

MACBETH

I am settled, and bend up
Each corporal agent to this terrible feat.
Away, and mock the time with fairest show:
False face must hide what the false heart doth know.

Exeunt

ACT II

SCENE I.

Court of Macbeth's castle.

Enter BANQUO, and FLEANCE bearing a torch before him

BANQUO
  How goes the night, boy?
FLEANCE
  The moon is down; I have not heard the clock.
BANQUO
  And she goes down at twelve.
FLEANCE
  I take't, 'tis later, sir.
BANQUO
  Hold, take my sword. There's husbandry in heaven;
  Their candles are all out. Take thee that too.
  A heavy summons lies like lead upon me,
  And yet I would not sleep: merciful powers,
  Restrain in me the cursed thoughts that nature
  Gives way to in repose!

Enter MACBETH, and a Servant with a torch

  Give me my sword.
  Who's there?
MACBETH
  A friend.
BANQUO
  What, sir, not yet at rest? The king's a-bed:
  He hath been in unusual pleasure, and
  Sent forth great largess to your offices.
  This diamond he greets your wife withal,

29

By the name of most kind hostess; and shut up
In measureless content.

MACBETH

Being unprepared,
Our will became the servant to defect;
Which else should free have wrought.

BANQUO

All's well.
I dreamt last night of the three weird sisters:
To you they have show'd some truth.

MACBETH

I think not of them:
Yet, when we can entreat an hour to serve,
We would spend it in some words upon that business,
If you would grant the time.

BANQUO

At your kind'st leisure.

MACBETH

If you shall cleave to my consent, when 'tis,
It shall make honour for you.

BANQUO

So I lose none
In seeking to augment it, but still keep
My bosom franchised and allegiance clear,
I shall be counsell'd.

MACBETH

Good repose the while!

BANQUO

Thanks, sir: the like to you!

Exeunt BANQUO and FLEANCE

MACBETH

Go bid thy mistress, when my drink is ready,
She strike upon the bell. Get thee to bed.

Exit Servant

Is this a dagger which I see before me,
The handle toward my hand? Come, let me clutch thee.
I have thee not, and yet I see thee still.
Art thou not, fatal vision, sensible
To feeling as to sight? or art thou but
A dagger of the mind, a false creation,
Proceeding from the heat-oppressed brain?
I see thee yet, in form as palpable
As this which now I draw.
Thou marshall'st me the way that I was going;
And such an instrument I was to use.
Mine eyes are made the fools o' the other senses,
Or else worth all the rest; I see thee still,
And on thy blade and dudgeon gouts of blood,
Which was not so before. There's no such thing:
It is the bloody business which informs
Thus to mine eyes. Now o'er the one halfworld
Nature seems dead, and wicked dreams abuse
The curtain'd sleep; witchcraft celebrates
Pale Hecate's offerings, and wither'd murder,
Alarum'd by his sentinel, the wolf,
Whose howl's his watch, thus with his stealthy pace.
With Tarquin's ravishing strides, towards his design
Moves like a ghost. Thou sure and firm-set earth,
Hear not my steps, which way they walk, for fear
Thy very stones prate of my whereabout,
And take the present horror from the time,
Which now suits with it. Whiles I threat, he lives:
Words to the heat of deeds too cold breath gives.

A bell rings

I go, and it is done; the bell invites me.

Hear it not, Duncan; for it is a knell
That summons thee to heaven or to hell.

Exit

SCENE II.

The same.

Enter LADY MACBETH

LADY MACBETH
That which hath made them drunk hath made me bold;
What hath quench'd them hath given me fire.
Hark! Peace!
It was the owl that shriek'd, the fatal bellman,
Which gives the stern'st good-night. He is about it:
The doors are open; and the surfeited grooms
Do mock their charge with snores: I have drugg'd
their possets,
That death and nature do contend about them,
Whether they live or die.
MACBETH
[Within] Who's there? what, ho!
LADY MACBETH
Alack, I am afraid they have awaked,
And 'tis not done. The attempt and not the deed
Confounds us. Hark! I laid their daggers ready;
He could not miss 'em. Had he not resembled
My father as he slept, I had done't.

Enter MACBETH

My husband!
MACBETH
I have done the deed. Didst thou not hear a noise?

LADY MACBETH
I heard the owl scream and the crickets cry.
Did not you speak?
MACBETH
When?
LADY MACBETH
Now.
MACBETH
As I descended?
LADY MACBETH
Ay.
MACBETH
Hark!
Who lies i' the second chamber?
LADY MACBETH
Donalbain.
MACBETH
This is a sorry sight.

Looking on his hands

LADY MACBETH
A foolish thought, to say a sorry sight.
MACBETH
There's one did laugh in's sleep, and one cried
'Murder!'
That they did wake each other: I stood and heard them:
But they did say their prayers, and address'd them
Again to sleep.
LADY MACBETH
There are two lodged together.
MACBETH
One cried 'God bless us!' and 'Amen' the other;
As they had seen me with these hangman's hands.
Listening their fear, I could not say 'Amen,'

When they did say 'God bless us!'
LADY MACBETH
Consider it not so deeply.
MACBETH
But wherefore could not I pronounce 'Amen'?
I had most need of blessing, and 'Amen'
Stuck in my throat.
LADY MACBETH
These deeds must not be thought
After these ways; so, it will make us mad.
MACBETH
Methought I heard a voice cry 'Sleep no more!
Macbeth does murder sleep', the innocent sleep,
Sleep that knits up the ravell'd sleeve of care,
The death of each day's life, sore labour's bath,
Balm of hurt minds, great nature's second course,
Chief nourisher in life's feast,--
LADY MACBETH
What do you mean?
MACBETH
Still it cried 'Sleep no more!' to all the house:
'Glamis hath murder'd sleep, and therefore Cawdor
Shall sleep no more; Macbeth shall sleep no more.'
LADY MACBETH
Who was it that thus cried? Why, worthy thane,
You do unbend your noble strength, to think
So brainsickly of things. Go get some water,
And wash this filthy witness from your hand.
Why did you bring these daggers from the place?
They must lie there: go carry them; and smear
The sleepy grooms with blood.
MACBETH
I'll go no more:
I am afraid to think what I have done;

Look on't again I dare not.
LADY MACBETH
Infirm of purpose!
Give me the daggers: the sleeping and the dead
Are but as pictures: 'tis the eye of childhood
That fears a painted devil. If he do bleed,
I'll gild the faces of the grooms withal;
For it must seem their guilt.

Exit. Knocking within

MACBETH
Whence is that knocking?
How is't with me, when every noise appals me?
What hands are here? ha! they pluck out mine eyes.
Will all great Neptune's ocean wash this blood
Clean from my hand? No, this my hand will rather
The multitudinous seas in incarnadine,
Making the green one red.

Re-enter LADY MACBETH

LADY MACBETH
My hands are of your colour; but I shame
To wear a heart so white.

Knocking within

I hear a knocking
At the south entry: retire we to our chamber;
A little water clears us of this deed:
How easy is it, then! Your constancy
Hath left you unattended.

Knocking within

Hark! more knocking.

Get on your nightgown, lest occasion call us,
And show us to be watchers. Be not lost
So poorly in your thoughts.
MACBETH
To know my deed, 'twere best not know myself.

Knocking within

Wake Duncan with thy knocking! I would thou couldst!

Exeunt

SCENE III.
The same.

Knocking within. Enter a Porter

Porter
Here's a knocking indeed! If a
man were porter of hell-gate, he should have
old turning the key.

Knocking within

Knock,
knock, knock! Who's there, i' the name of
Beelzebub? Here's a farmer, that hanged
himself on the expectation of plenty: come in
time; have napkins enow about you; here
you'll sweat for't.

Knocking within

Knock,
knock! Who's there, in the other devil's
name? Faith, here's an equivocator, that could
swear in both the scales against either scale;

who committed treason enough for God's sake,
yet could not equivocate to heaven: O, come
in, equivocator.

Knocking within

Knock,
knock, knock! Who's there? Faith, here's an
English tailor come hither, for stealing out of
a French hose: come in, tailor; here you may
roast your goose.

Knocking within

Knock,
knock; never at quiet! What are you? But
this place is too cold for hell. I'll devil-porter
it no further: I had thought to have let in
some of all professions that go the primrose
way to the everlasting bonfire.

Knocking within

Anon, anon! I pray you, remember the porter.

Opens the gate

Enter MACDUFF and LENNOX

MACDUFF
Was it so late, friend, ere you went to bed,
That you do lie so late?
Porter
'Faith sir, we were carousing till the
second cock: and drink, sir, is a great
provoker of three things.

MACDUFF

What three things does drink especially provoke?

Porter

Marry, sir, nose-painting, sleep, and
urine. Lechery, sir, it provokes, and unprovokes;
it provokes the desire, but it takes
away the performance: therefore, much drink
may be said to be an equivocator with lechery:
it makes him, and it mars him; it sets
him on, and it takes him off; it persuades him,
and disheartens him; makes him stand to, and
not stand to; in conclusion, equivocates him
in a sleep, and, giving him the lie, leaves him.

MACDUFF

I believe drink gave thee the lie last night.

Porter

That it did, sir, i' the very throat on
me: but I requited him for his lie; and, I
think, being too strong for him, though he took
up my legs sometime, yet I made a shift to cast
him.

MACDUFF

Is thy master stirring?

Enter MACBETH

Our knocking has awaked him; here he comes.

LENNOX

Good morrow, noble sir.

MACBETH

Good morrow, both.

MACDUFF

Is the king stirring, worthy thane?

MACBETH

Not yet.

MACDUFF
He did command me to call timely on him:
I have almost slipp'd the hour.
MACBETH
I'll bring you to him.
MACDUFF
I know this is a joyful trouble to you;
But yet 'tis one.
MACBETH
The labour we delight in physics pain.
This is the door.
MACDUFF
I'll make so bold to call,
For 'tis my limited service.

Exit

LENNOX
Goes the king hence to-day?
MACBETH
He does: he did appoint so.
LENNOX
The night has been unruly: where we lay,
Our chimneys were blown down; and, as they say,
Lamentings heard i' the air; strange screams of death,
And prophesying with accents terrible
Of dire combustion and confused events
New hatch'd to the woeful time: the obscure bird
Clamour'd the livelong night: some say, the earth
Was feverous and did shake.
MACBETH
'Twas a rough night.
LENNOX
My young remembrance cannot parallel
A fellow to it.

Re-enter MACDUFF

MACDUFF
O horror, horror, horror! Tongue nor heart
Cannot conceive nor name thee!
MACBETH LENNOX
What's the matter.
MACDUFF
Confusion now hath made his masterpiece!
Most sacrilegious murder hath broke ope
The Lord's anointed temple, and stole thence
The life o' the building!
MACBETH
What is 't you say? the life?
LENNOX
Mean you his majesty?
MACDUFF
Approach the chamber, and destroy your sight
With a new Gorgon: do not bid me speak;
See, and then speak yourselves.

Exeunt MACBETH and LENNOX

Awake, awake!
Ring the alarum-bell. Murder and treason!
Banquo and Donalbain! Malcolm! awake!
Shake off this downy sleep, death's counterfeit,
And look on death itself! up, up, and see
The great doom's image! Malcolm! Banquo!
As from your graves rise up, and walk like sprites,
To countenance this horror! Ring the bell.

Bell rings

Enter LADY MACBETH

LADY MACBETH
What's the business,
That such a hideous trumpet calls to parley
The sleepers of the house? speak, speak!
MACDUFF
O gentle lady,
'Tis not for you to hear what I can speak:
The repetition, in a woman's ear,
Would murder as it fell.

Enter BANQUO

O Banquo, Banquo,
Our royal master 's murder'd!
LADY MACBETH
Woe, alas!
What, in our house?
BANQUO
Too cruel any where.
Dear Duff, I prithee, contradict thyself,
And say it is not so.

Re-enter MACBETH and LENNOX, with ROSS

MACBETH
Had I but died an hour before this chance,
I had lived a blessed time; for, from this instant,
There 's nothing serious in mortality:
All is but toys: renown and grace is dead;
The wine of life is drawn, and the mere lees
Is left this vault to brag of.

Enter MALCOLM and DONALBAIN

DONALBAIN

What is amiss?
MACBETH
You are, and do not know't:
The spring, the head, the fountain of your blood
Is stopp'd; the very source of it is stopp'd.
MACDUFF
Your royal father 's murder'd.
MALCOLM
O, by whom?
LENNOX
Those of his chamber, as it seem'd, had done 't:
Their hands and faces were an badged with blood;
So were their daggers, which unwiped we found
Upon their pillows:
They stared, and were distracted; no man's life
Was to be trusted with them.
MACBETH
O, yet I do repent me of my fury,
That I did kill them.
MACDUFF
Wherefore did you so?
MACBETH
Who can be wise, amazed, temperate and furious,
Loyal and neutral, in a moment? No man:
The expedition my violent love
Outrun the pauser, reason. Here lay Duncan,
His silver skin laced with his golden blood;
And his gash'd stabs look'd like a breach in nature
For ruin's wasteful entrance: there, the murderers,
Steep'd in the colours of their trade, their daggers
Unmannerly breech'd with gore: who could refrain,
That had a heart to love, and in that heart
Courage to make 's love kno wn?
LADY MACBETH

Help me hence, ho!
MACDUFF
  Look to the lady.
MALCOLM
  [Aside to DONALBAIN] Why do we hold our tongues,
    That most may claim this argument for ours?
DONALBAIN
  [Aside to MALCOLM] What should be spoken here,
    where our fate,
    Hid in an auger-hole, may rush, and seize us?
    Let 's away;
    Our tears are not yet brew'd.
MALCOLM
  [Aside to DONALBAIN] Nor our strong sorrow
    Upon the foot of motion.
BANQUO
  Look to the lady:

            LADY MACBETH is carried out

  And when we have our naked frailties hid,
  That suffer in exposure, let us meet,
  And question this most bloody piece of work,
  To know it further. Fears and scruples shake us:
  In the great hand of God I stand; and thence
  Against the undivulged pretence I fight
  Of treasonous malice.
MACDUFF
  And so do I.
ALL
  So all.
MACBETH
  Let's briefly put on manly readiness,
  And meet i' the hall together.
ALL

Well contented.

Exeunt all but Malcolm and Donalbain.

MALCOLM
> What will you do? Let's not consort with them:
> To show an unfelt sorrow is an office
> Which the false man does easy. I'll to England.

DONALBAIN
> To Ireland, I; our separated fortune
> Shall keep us both the safer: where we are,
> There's daggers in men's smiles: the near in blood,
> The nearer bloody.

MALCOLM
> This murderous shaft that's shot
> Hath not yet lighted, and our safest way
> Is to avoid the aim. Therefore, to horse;
> And let us not be dainty of leave-taking,
> But shift away: there's warrant in that theft
> Which steals itself, when there's no mercy left.

Exeunt

SCENE IV.

Outside Macbeth's castle.

Enter ROSS and an old Man

Old Man
> Threescore and ten I can remember well:
> Within the volume of which time I have seen
> Hours dreadful and things strange; but this sore night
> Hath trifled former knowings.

ROSS
> Ah, good father,

Thou seest, the heavens, as troubled with man's act,
Threaten his bloody stage: by the clock, 'tis day,
And yet dark night strangles the travelling lamp:
Is't night's predominance, or the day's shame,
That darkness does the face of earth entomb,
When living light should kiss it?

Old Man
'Tis unnatural,
Even like the deed that's done. On Tuesday last,
A falcon, towering in her pride of place,
Was by a mousing owl hawk'd at and kill'd.

ROSS
And Duncan's horses--a thing most strange and certain--
Beauteous and swift, the minions of their race,
Turn'd wild in nature, broke their stalls, flung out,
Contending 'gainst obedience, as they would make
War with mankind.

Old Man
'Tis said they eat each other.

ROSS
They did so, to the amazement of mine eyes
That look'd upon't. Here comes the good Macduff.

Enter MACDUFF

How goes the world, sir, now?

MACDUFF
Why, see you not?

ROSS
Is't known who did this more than bloody deed?

MACDUFF
Those that Macbeth hath slain.

ROSS
Alas, the day!
What good could they pretend?

MACDUFF
They were suborn'd:
Malcolm and Donalbain, the king's two sons,
Are stol'n away and fled; which puts upon them
Suspicion of the deed.
ROSS
'Gainst nature still!
Thriftless ambition, that wilt ravin up
Thine own life's means! Then 'tis most like
The sovereignty will fall upon Macbeth.
MACDUFF
He is already named, and gone to Scone
To be invested.
ROSS
Where is Duncan's body?
MACDUFF
Carried to Colmekill,
The sacred storehouse of his predecessors,
And guardian of their bones.
ROSS
Will you to Scone?
MACDUFF
No, cousin, I'll to Fife.
ROSS
Well, I will thither.
MACDUFF
Well, may you see things well done there: adieu!
Lest our old robes sit easier than our new!
ROSS
Farewell, father.
Old Man
God's benison go with you; and with those
That would make good of bad, and friends of foes!

Exeunt

ACT III

SCENE I.

Forres. The palace.

Enter BANQUO

BANQUO
　Thou hast it now: king, Cawdor, Glamis, all,
　As the weird women promised, and, I fear,
　Thou play'dst most foully for't: yet it was said
　It should not stand in thy posterity,
　But that myself should be the root and father
　Of many kings. If there come truth from them--
　As upon thee, Macbeth, their speeches shine--
　Why, by the verities on thee made good,
　May they not be my oracles as well,
　And set me up in hope? But hush! no more.

　　　Sennet sounded. Enter MACBETH, as king, LADY
　MACBETH, as queen, LENNOX, ROSS, Lords, Ladies, and
　　　　　　　　Attendants

MACBETH
　Here's our chief guest.
LADY MACBETH
　If he had been forgotten,
　It had been as a gap in our great feast,
　And all-thing unbecoming.
MACBETH
　To-night we hold a solemn supper sir,
　And I'll request your presence.
BANQUO
　Let your highness

Command upon me; to the which my duties
Are with a most indissoluble tie
For ever knit.

MACBETH
Ride you this afternoon?

BANQUO
Ay, my good lord.

MACBETH
We should have else desired your good advice,
Which still hath been both grave and prosperous,
In this day's council; but we'll take to-morrow.
Is't far you ride?

BANQUO
As far, my lord, as will fill up the time
'Twixt this and supper: go not my horse the better,
I must become a borrower of the night
For a dark hour or twain.

MACBETH
Fail not our feast.

BANQUO
My lord, I will not.

MACBETH
We hear, our bloody cousins are bestow'd
In England and in Ireland, not confessing
Their cruel parricide, filling their hearers
With strange invention: but of that to-morrow,
When therewithal we shall have cause of state
Craving us jointly. Hie you to horse: adieu,
Till you return at night. Goes Fleance with you?

BANQUO
Ay, my good lord: our time does call upon 's.

MACBETH
I wish your horses swift and sure of foot;
And so I do commend you to their backs. Farewell.

Exit BANQUO

Let every man be master of his time
Till seven at night: to make society
The sweeter welcome, we will keep ourself
Till supper-time alone: while then, God be with you!

Exeunt all but MACBETH, and an attendant

Sirrah, a word with you: attend those men
Our pleasure?
ATTENDANT
They are, my lord, without the palace gate.
MACBETH
Bring them before us.

Exit Attendant

To be thus is nothing;
But to be safely thus.--Our fears in Banquo
Stick deep; and in his royalty of nature
Reigns that which would be fear'd: 'tis much he dares;
And, to that dauntless temper of his mind,
He hath a wisdom that doth guide his valour
To act in safety. There is none but he
Whose being I do fear: and, under him,
My Genius is rebuked; as, it is said,
Mark Antony's was by Caesar. He chid the sisters
When first they put the name of king upon me,
And bade them speak to him: then prophet-like
They hail'd him father to a line of kings:
Upon my head they placed a fruitless crown,
And put a barren sceptre in my gripe,
Thence to be wrench'd with an unlineal hand,
No son of mine succeeding. If 't be so,

For Banquo's issue have I filed my mind;
For them the gracious Duncan have I murder'd;
Put rancours in the vessel of my peace
Only for them; and mine eternal jewel
Given to the common enemy of man,
To make them kings, the seed of Banquo kings!
Rather than so, come fate into the list.
And champion me to the utterance! Who's there!

Re-enter Attendant, with two Murderers

Now go to the door, and stay there till we call.

Exit Attendant

Was it not yesterday we spoke together?
First Murderer
It was, so please your highness.
MACBETH
Well then, now
Have you consider'd of my speeches? Know
That it was he in the times past which held you
So under fortune, which you thought had been
Our innocent self: this I made good to you
In our last conference, pass'd in probation with you,
How you were borne in hand, how cross'd,
the instruments,
Who wrought with them, and all things else that might
To half a soul and to a notion crazed
Say 'Thus did Banquo.'
First Murderer
You made it known to us.
MACBETH
I did so, and went further, which is now
Our point of second meeting. Do you find

Your patience so predominant in your nature
That you can let this go? Are you so gospell'd
To pray for this good man and for his issue,
Whose heavy hand hath bow'd you to the grave
And beggar'd yours for ever?
First Murderer
We are men, my liege.
MACBETH
Ay, in the catalogue ye go for men;
As hounds and greyhounds, mongrels, spaniels, curs,
Shoughs, water-rugs and demi-wolves, are clept
All by the name of dogs: the valued file
Distinguishes the swift, the slow, the subtle,
The housekeeper, the hunter, every one
According to the gift which bounteous nature
Hath in him closed; whereby he does receive
Particular addition. from the bill
That writes them all alike: and so of men.
Now, if you have a station in the file,
Not i' the worst rank of manhood, say 't;
And I will put that business in your bosoms,
Whose execution takes your enemy off,
Grapples you to the heart and love of us,
Who wear our health but sickly in his life,
Which in his death were perfect.
Second Murderer
I am one, my liege,
Whom the vile blows and buffets of the world
Have so incensed that I am reckless what
I do to spite the world.
First Murderer
And I another
So weary with disasters, tugg'd with fortune,
That I would set my lie on any chance,

To mend it, or be rid on't.
MACBETH
Both of you
Know Banquo was your enemy.
Both Murderers
True, my lord.
MACBETH
So is he mine; and in such bloody distance,
That every minute of his being thrusts
Against my near'st of life: and though I could
With barefaced power sweep him from my sight
And bid my will avouch it, yet I must not,
For certain friends that are both his and mine,
Whose loves I may not drop, but wail his fall
Who I myself struck down; and thence it is,
That I to your assistance do make love,
Masking the business from the common eye
For sundry weighty reasons.
Second Murderer
We shall, my lord,
Perform what you command us.
First Murderer
Though our lives--
MACBETH
Your spirits shine through you. Within this hour at most
I will advise you where to plant yourselves;
Acquaint you with the perfect spy o' the time,
The moment on't; for't must be done to-night,
And something from the palace; always thought
That I require a clearness: and with him--
To leave no rubs nor botches in the work--
Fleance his son, that keeps him company,
Whose absence is no less material to me
Than is his father's, must embrace the fate

Of that dark hour. Resolve yourselves apart:
I'll come to you anon.
Both Murderers
We are resolved, my lord.
MACBETH
I'll call upon you straight: abide within.

Exeunt Murderers

It is concluded. Banquo, thy soul's flight,
If it find heaven, must find it out to-night.

Exit

SCENE II.

The palace.

Enter LADY MACBETH and a Servant

LADY MACBETH
Is Banquo gone from court?
Servant
Ay, madam, but returns again to-night.
LADY MACBETH
Say to the king, I would attend his leisure
For a few words.
Servant
Madam, I will.

Exit

LADY MACBETH
Nought's had, all's spent,
Where our desire is got without content:
'Tis safer to be that which we destroy
Than by destruction dwell in doubtful joy.

Enter MACBETH

How now, my lord! why do you keep alone,
Of sorriest fancies your companions making,
Using those thoughts which should indeed have died
With them they think on? Things without all remedy
Should be without regard: what's done is done.

MACBETH
We have scotch'd the snake, not kill'd it:
She'll close and be herself, whilst our poor malice
Remains in danger of her former tooth.
But let the frame of things disjoint, both the
worlds suffer,
Ere we will eat our meal in fear and sleep
In the affliction of these terrible dreams
That shake us nightly: better be with the dead,
Whom we, to gain our peace, have sent to peace,
Than on the torture of the mind to lie
In restless ecstasy. Duncan is in his grave;
After life's fitful fever he sleeps well;
Treason has done his worst: nor steel, nor poison,
Malice domestic, foreign levy, nothing,
Can touch him further.

LADY MACBETH
Come on;
Gentle my lord, sleek o'er your rugged looks;
Be bright and jovial among your guests to-night.

MACBETH
So shall I, love; and so, I pray, be you:
Let your remembrance apply to Banquo;
Present him eminence, both with eye and tongue:
Unsafe the while, that we
Must lave our honours in these flattering streams,
And make our faces vizards to our hearts,

Disguising what they are.
LADY MACBETH
You must leave this.
MACBETH
O, full of scorpions is my mind, dear wife!
Thou know'st that Banquo, and his Fleance, lives.
LADY MACBETH
But in them nature's copy's not eterne.
MACBETH
There's comfort yet; they are assailable;
Then be thou jocund: ere the bat hath flown
His cloister'd flight, ere to black Hecate's summons
The shard-borne beetle with his drowsy hums
Hath rung night's yawning peal, there shall be done
A deed of dreadful note.
LADY MACBETH
What's to be done?
MACBETH
Be innocent of the knowledge, dearest chuck,
Till thou applaud the deed. Come, seeling night,
Scarf up the tender eye of pitiful day;
And with thy bloody and invisible hand
Cancel and tear to pieces that great bond
Which keeps me pale! Light thickens; and the crow
Makes wing to the rooky wood:
Good things of day begin to droop and drowse;
While night's black agents to their preys do rouse.
Thou marvell'st at my words: but hold thee still;
Things bad begun make strong themselves by ill.
So, prithee, go with me.

Exeunt

SCENE III.

A park near the palace.

Enter three Murderers

First Murderer
But who did bid thee join with us?
Third Murderer
Macbeth.
Second Murderer
He needs not our mistrust, since he delivers
Our offices and what we have to do
To the direction just.
First Murderer
Then stand with us.
The west yet glimmers with some streaks of day:
Now spurs the lated traveller apace
To gain the timely inn; and near approaches
The subject of our watch.
Third Murderer
Hark! I hear horses.
BANQUO
[Within] Give us a light there, ho!
Second Murderer
Then 'tis he: the rest
That are within the note of expectation
Already are i' the court.
First Murderer
His horses go about.
Third Murderer
Almost a mile: but he does usually,
So all men do, from hence to the palace gate
Make it their walk.
Second Murderer
A light, a light!

Enter BANQUO, and FLEANCE with a torch

Third Murderer
  'Tis he.
First Murderer
  Stand to't.
BANQUO
  It will be rain to-night.
First Murderer
  Let it come down.

They set upon BANQUO

BANQUO
  O, treachery! Fly, good Fleance, fly, fly, fly!
  Thou mayst revenge. O slave!

Dies. FLEANCE escapes

Third Murderer
  Who did strike out the light?
First Murderer
  Wast not the way?
Third Murderer
  There's but one down; the son is fled.
Second Murderer
  We have lost
  Best half of our affair.
First Murderer
  Well, let's away, and say how much is done.

Exeunt

SCENE IV.

The same. Hall in the palace.

*A banquet prepared. Enter MACBETH, LADY MACBETH,
ROSS, LENNOX, Lords, and Attendants*

MACBETH
> You know your own degrees; sit down: at first
> And last the hearty welcome.

Lords
> Thanks to your majesty.

MACBETH
> Ourself will mingle with society,
> And play the humble host.
> Our hostess keeps her state, but in best time
> We will require her welcome.

LADY MACBETH
> Pronounce it for me, sir, to all our friends;
> For my heart speaks they are welcome.

First Murderer appears at the door

MACBETH
> See, they encounter thee with their hearts' thanks.
> Both sides are even: here I'll sit i' the midst:
> Be large in mirth; anon we'll drink a measure
> The table round.

Approaching the door

> There's blood on thy face.

First Murderer
> 'Tis Banquo's then.

MACBETH
> 'Tis better thee without than he within.
> Is he dispatch'd?

First Murderer
  My lord, his throat is cut; that I did for him.
MACBETH
  Thou art the best o' the cut-throats: yet he's good
  That did the like for Fleance: if thou didst it,
  Thou art the nonpareil.
First Murderer
  Most royal sir,
  Fleance is 'scaped.
MACBETH
  Then comes my fit again: I had else been perfect,
  Whole as the marble, founded as the rock,
  As broad and general as the casing air:
  But now I am cabin'd, cribb'd, confined, bound in
  To saucy doubts and fears. But Banquo's safe?
First Murderer
  Ay, my good lord: safe in a ditch he bides,
  With twenty trenched gashes on his head;
  The least a death to nature.
MACBETH
  Thanks for that:
  There the grown serpent lies; the worm that's fled
  Hath nature that in time will venom breed,
  No teeth for the present. Get thee gone: to-morrow
  We'll hear, ourselves, again.

                    Exit Murderer

LADY MACBETH
  My royal lord,
  You do not give the cheer: the feast is sold
  That is not often vouch'd, while 'tis a-making,
  'Tis given with welcome: to feed were best at home;
  From thence the sauce to meat is ceremony;
  Meeting were bare without it.

MACBETH
Sweet remembrancer!
Now, good digestion wait on appetite,
And health on both!
LENNOX
May't please your highness sit.

The GHOST OF BANQUO enters, and sits in MACBETH's place

MACBETH
Here had we now our country's honour roof'd,
Were the graced person of our Banquo present;
Who may I rather challenge for unkindness
Than pity for mischance!
ROSS
His absence, sir,
Lays blame upon his promise. Please't your highness
To grace us with your royal company.
MACBETH
The table's full.
LENNOX
Here is a place reserved, sir.
MACBETH
Where?
LENNOX
Here, my good lord. What is't that moves your
highness?
MACBETH
Which of you have done this?
Lords
What, my good lord?
MACBETH
Thou canst not say I did it: never shake
Thy gory locks at me.

ROSS
Gentlemen, rise: his highness is not well.
LADY MACBETH
Sit, worthy friends: my lord is often thus,
And hath been from his youth: pray you, keep seat;
The fit is momentary; upon a thought
He will again be well: if much you note him,
You shall offend him and extend his passion:
Feed, and regard him not. Are you a man?
MACBETH
Ay, and a bold one, that dare look on that
Which might appal the devil.
LADY MACBETH
O proper stuff!
This is the very painting of your fear:
This is the air-drawn dagger which, you said,
Led you to Duncan. O, these flaws and starts,
Impostors to true fear, would well become
A woman's story at a winter's fire,
Authorized by her grandam. Shame itself!
Why do you make such faces? When all's done,
You look but on a stool.
MACBETH
Prithee, see there! behold! look! lo!
how say you?
Why, what care I? If thou canst nod, speak too.
If charnel-houses and our graves must send
Those that we bury back, our monuments
Shall be the maws of kites.

GHOST OF BANQUO vanishes

LADY MACBETH
What, quite unmann'd in folly?
MACBETH

If I stand here, I saw him.
LADY MACBETH
Fie, for shame!
MACBETH
Blood hath been shed ere now, i' the olden time,
Ere human statute purged the gentle weal;
Ay, and since too, murders have been perform'd
Too terrible for the ear: the times have been,
That, when the brains were out, the man would die,
And there an end; but now they rise again,
With twenty mortal murders on their crowns,
And push us from our stools: this is more strange
Than such a murder is.
LADY MACBETH
My worthy lord,
Your noble friends do lack you.
MACBETH
I do forget.
Do not muse at me, my most worthy friends,
I have a strange infirmity, which is nothing
To those that know me. Come, love and health to all;
Then I'll sit down. Give me some wine; fill full.
I drink to the general joy o' the whole table,
And to our dear friend Banquo, whom we miss;
Would he were here! to all, and him, we thirst,
And all to all.
Lords
Our duties, and the pledge.

Re-enter GHOST OF BANQUO

MACBETH
Avaunt! and quit my sight! let the earth hide thee!
Thy bones are marrowless, thy blood is cold;
Thou hast no speculation in those eyes

Which thou dost glare with!
LADY MACBETH
Think of this, good peers,
But as a thing of custom: 'tis no other;
Only it spoils the pleasure of the time.
MACBETH
What man dare, I dare:
Approach thou like the rugged Russian bear,
The arm'd rhinoceros, or the Hyrcan tiger;
Take any shape but that, and my firm nerves
Shall never tremble: or be alive again,
And dare me to the desert with thy sword;
If trembling I inhabit then, protest me
The baby of a girl. Hence, horrible shadow!
Unreal mockery, hence!

GHOST OF BANQUO vanishes

Why, so: being gone,
I am a man again. Pray you, sit still.
LADY MACBETH
You have displaced the mirth, broke the good meeting,
With most admired disorder.
MACBETH
Can such things be,
And overcome us like a summer's cloud,
Without our special wonder? You make me strange
Even to the disposition that I owe,
When now I think you can behold such sights,
And keep the natural ruby of your cheeks,
When mine is blanched with fear.
ROSS
What sights, my lord?
LADY MACBETH
I pray you, speak not; he grows worse and worse;

Question enrages him. At once, good night:
Stand not upon the order of your going,
But go at once.
LENNOX
Good night; and better health
Attend his majesty!
LADY MACBETH
A kind good night to all!

Exeunt all but MACBETH and LADY MACBETH

MACBETH
It will have blood; they say, blood will have blood:
Stones have been known to move and trees to speak;
Augurs and understood relations have
By magot-pies and choughs and rooks brought forth
The secret'st man of blood. What is the night?
LADY MACBETH
Almost at odds with morning, which is which.
MACBETH
How say'st thou, that Macduff denies his person
At our great bidding?
LADY MACBETH
Did you send to him, sir?
MACBETH
I hear it by the way; but I will send:
There's not a one of them but in his house
I keep a servant fee'd. I will to-morrow,
And betimes I will, to the weird sisters:
More shall they speak; for now I am bent to know,
By the worst means, the worst. For mine own good,
All causes shall give way: I am in blood
Stepp'd in so far that, should I wade no more,
Returning were as tedious as go o'er:
Strange things I have in head, that will to hand;

Which must be acted ere they may be scann'd.
LADY MACBETH
You lack the season of all natures, sleep.
MACBETH
Come, we'll to sleep. My strange and self-abuse
Is the initiate fear that wants hard use:
We are yet but young in deed.

Exeunt

SCENE V.

A Heath.

Thunder. Enter the three Witches meeting HECATE

First Witch
Why, how now, Hecate! you look angerly.
HECATE
Have I not reason, beldams as you are,
Saucy and overbold? How did you dare
To trade and traffic with Macbeth
In riddles and affairs of death;
And I, the mistress of your charms,
The close contriver of all harms,
Was never call'd to bear my part,
Or show the glory of our art?
And, which is worse, all you have done
Hath been but for a wayward son,
Spiteful and wrathful, who, as others do,
Loves for his own ends, not for you.
But make amends now: get you gone,
And at the pit of Acheron
Meet me i' the morning: thither he
Will come to know his destiny:
Your vessels and your spells provide,

Your charms and every thing beside.
I am for the air; this night I'll spend
Unto a dismal and a fatal end:
Great business must be wrought ere noon:
Upon the corner of the moon
There hangs a vaporous drop profound;
I'll catch it ere it come to ground:
And that distill'd by magic sleights
Shall raise such artificial sprites
As by the strength of their illusion
Shall draw him on to his confusion:
He shall spurn fate, scorn death, and bear
He hopes 'bove wisdom, grace and fear:
And you all know, security
Is mortals' chiefest enemy.

Music and a song within: 'Come away, come away,' & c

Hark! I am call'd; my little spirit, see,
Sits in a foggy cloud, and stays for me.

Exit

First Witch
Come, let's make haste; she'll soon be back again.

Exeunt

SCENE VI.
Forres. The palace.

Enter LENNOX and another Lord

LENNOX
My former speeches have but hit your thoughts,
Which can interpret further: only, I say,

Things have been strangely borne. The
gracious Duncan
Was pitied of Macbeth: marry, he was dead:
And the right-valiant Banquo walk'd too late;
Whom, you may say, if't please you, Fleance kill'd,
For Fleance fled: men must not walk too late.
Who cannot want the thought how monstrous
It was for Malcolm and for Donalbain
To kill their gracious father? damned fact!
How it did grieve Macbeth! did he not straight
In pious rage the two delinquents tear,
That were the slaves of drink and thralls of sleep?
Was not that nobly done? Ay, and wisely too;
For 'twould have anger'd any heart alive
To hear the men deny't. So that, I say,
He has borne all things well: and I do think
That had he Duncan's sons under his key--
As, an't please heaven, he shall not--they
should find
What 'twere to kill a father; so should Fleance.
But, peace! for from broad words and 'cause he fail'd
His presence at the tyrant's feast, I hear
Macduff lives in disgrace: sir, can you tell
Where he bestows himself?
Lord
    The son of Duncan,
From whom this tyrant holds the due of birth
Lives in the English court, and is received
Of the most pious Edward with such grace
That the malevolence of fortune nothing
Takes from his high respect: thither Macduff
Is gone to pray the holy king, upon his aid
To wake Northumberland and warlike Siward:
That, by the help of these--with Him above

To ratify the work--we may again
Give to our tables meat, sleep to our nights,
Free from our feasts and banquets bloody knives,
Do faithful homage and receive free honours:
All which we pine for now: and this report
Hath so exasperate the king that he
Prepares for some attempt of war.

LENNOX

Sent he to Macduff?

Lord

He did: and with an absolute 'Sir, not I,'
The cloudy messenger turns me his back,
And hums, as who should say 'You'll rue the time
That clogs me with this answer.'

LENNOX

And that well might
Advise him to a caution, to hold what distance
His wisdom can provide. Some holy angel
Fly to the court of England and unfold
His message ere he come, that a swift blessing
May soon return to this our suffering country
Under a hand accursed!

Lord

I'll send my prayers with him.

Exeunt

ACT IV

SCENE I.

A cavern. In the middle, a boiling cauldron.

Thunder. Enter the three Witches

First Witch
   Thrice the brinded cat hath mew'd.
Second Witch
   Thrice and once the hedge-pig whined.
Third Witch
   Harpier cries 'Tis time, 'tis time.
First Witch
   Round about the cauldron go;
   In the poison'd entrails throw.
   Toad, that under cold stone
   Days and nights has thirty-one
   Swelter'd venom sleeping got,
   Boil thou first i' the charmed pot.
ALL
   Double, double toil and trouble;
   Fire burn, and cauldron bubble.
Second Witch
   Fillet of a fenny snake,
   In the cauldron boil and bake;
   Eye of newt and toe of frog,
   Wool of bat and tongue of dog,
   Adder's fork and blind-worm's sting,
   Lizard's leg and owlet's wing,
   For a charm of powerful trouble,
   Like a hell-broth boil and bubble.
ALL
   Double, double toil and trouble;

Fire burn and cauldron bubble.
Third Witch
    Scale of dragon, tooth of wolf,
    Witches' mummy, maw and gulf
    Of the ravin'd salt-sea shark,
    Root of hemlock digg'd i' the dark,
    Liver of blaspheming Jew,
    Gall of goat, and slips of yew
    Silver'd in the moon's eclipse,
    Nose of Turk and Tartar's lips,
    Finger of birth-strangled babe
    Ditch-deliver'd by a drab,
    Make the gruel thick and slab:
    Add thereto a tiger's chaudron,
    For the ingredients of our cauldron.
ALL
    Double, double toil and trouble;
    Fire burn and cauldron bubble.
Second Witch
    Cool it with a baboon's blood,
    Then the charm is firm and good.

Enter HECATE to the other three Witches

HECATE
    O well done! I commend your pains;
    And every one shall share i' the gains;
    And now about the cauldron sing,
    Live elves and fairies in a ring,
    Enchanting all that you put in.

Music and a song: 'Black spirits,' & c

HECATE retires

Second Witch
    By the pricking of my thumbs,
    Something wicked this way comes.
    Open, locks,
    Whoever knocks!

Enter MACBETH

MACBETH
    How now, you secret, black, and midnight hags!
    What is't you do?
ALL
    A deed without a name.
MACBETH
    I conjure you, by that which you profess,
    Howe'er you come to know it, answer me:
    Though you untie the winds and let them fight
    Against the churches; though the yesty waves
    Confound and swallow navigation up;
    Though bladed corn be lodged and trees blown down;
    Though castles topple on their warders' heads;
    Though palaces and pyramids do slope
    Their heads to their foundations; though the treasure
    Of nature's germens tumble all together,
    Even till destruction sicken; answer me
    To what I ask you.
First Witch
    Speak.
Second Witch
    Demand.
Third Witch
    We'll answer.
First Witch
    Say, if thou'dst rather hear it from our mouths,
    Or from our masters?

MACBETH
Call 'em; let me see 'em.
First Witch
Pour in sow's blood, that hath eaten
Her nine farrow; grease that's sweaten
From the murderer's gibbet throw
Into the flame.
ALL
Come, high or low;
Thyself and office deftly show!

Thunder. First Apparition: an armed Head

MACBETH
Tell me, thou unknown power,--
First Witch
He knows thy thought:
Hear his speech, but say thou nought.
First Apparition
Macbeth! Macbeth! Macbeth! beware Macduff;
Beware the thane of Fife. Dismiss me. Enough.

Descends

MACBETH
Whate'er thou art, for thy good caution, thanks;
Thou hast harp'd my fear aright: but one
word more,--
First Witch
He will not be commanded: here's another,
More potent than the first.

Thunder. Second Apparition: A bloody Child

Second Apparition
Macbeth! Macbeth! Macbeth!

MACBETH
Had I three ears, I'ld hear thee.
Second Apparition
Be bloody, bold, and resolute; laugh to scorn
The power of man, for none of woman born
Shall harm Macbeth.

Descends

MACBETH
Then live, Macduff: what need I fear of thee?
But yet I'll make assurance double sure,
And take a bond of fate: thou shalt not live;
That I may tell pale-hearted fear it lies,
And sleep in spite of thunder.

Thunder. Third Apparition: a Child crowned, with a tree in his hand

What is this
That rises like the issue of a king,
And wears upon his baby-brow the round
And top of sovereignty?
ALL
Listen, but speak not to't.
Third Apparition
Be lion-mettled, proud; and take no care
Who chafes, who frets, or where conspirers are:
Macbeth shall never vanquish'd be until
Great Birnam wood to high Dunsinane hill
Shall come against him.

Descends

MACBETH
That will never be

Who can impress the forest, bid the tree
Unfix his earth-bound root? Sweet bodements! good!
Rebellion's head, rise never till the wood
Of Birnam rise, and our high-placed Macbeth
Shall live the lease of nature, pay his breath
To time and mortal custom. Yet my heart
Throbs to know one thing: tell me, if your art
Can tell so much: shall Banquo's issue ever
Reign in this kingdom?

ALL
Seek to know no more.

MACBETH
I will be satisfied: deny me this,
And an eternal curse fall on you! Let me know.
Why sinks that cauldron? and what noise is this?

Hautboys

First Witch
Show!
Second Witch
Show!
Third Witch
Show!
ALL
Show his eyes, and grieve his heart;
Come like shadows, so depart!

A show of Eight Kings, the last with a glass in his hand;
GHOST OF BANQUO following

MACBETH
Thou art too like the spirit of Banquo: down!
Thy crown does sear mine eye-balls. And thy hair,
Thou other gold-bound brow, is like the first.

A third is like the former. Filthy hags!
Why do you show me this? A fourth! Start, eyes!
What, will the line stretch out to the crack of doom?
Another yet! A seventh! I'll see no more:
And yet the eighth appears, who bears a glass
Which shows me many more; and some I see
That two-fold balls and treble scepters carry:
Horrible sight! Now, I see, 'tis true;
For the blood-bolter'd Banquo smiles upon me,
And points at them for his.

Apparitions vanish

What, is this so?
First Witch
Ay, sir, all this is so: but why
Stands Macbeth thus amazedly?
Come, sisters, cheer we up his sprites,
And show the best of our delights:
I'll charm the air to give a sound,
While you perform your antic round:
That this great king may kindly say,
Our duties did his welcome pay.

Music. The witches dance and then vanish, with HECATE

MACBETH
Where are they? Gone? Let this pernicious hour
Stand aye accursed in the calendar!
Come in, without there!

Enter LENNOX

LENNOX
What's your grace's will?
MACBETH

Saw you the weird sisters?
LENNOX
No, my lord.
MACBETH
Came they not by you?
LENNOX
No, indeed, my lord.
MACBETH
Infected be the air whereon they ride;
And damn'd all those that trust them! I did hear
The galloping of horse: who was't came by?
LENNOX
'Tis two or three, my lord, that bring you word
Macduff is fled to England.
MACBETH
Fled to England!
LENNOX
Ay, my good lord.
MACBETH
Time, thou anticipatest my dread exploits:
The flighty purpose never is o'ertook
Unless the deed go with it; from this moment
The very firstlings of my heart shall be
The firstlings of my hand. And even now,
To crown my thoughts with acts, be it thought and done:
The castle of Macduff I will surprise;
Seize upon Fife; give to the edge o' the sword
His wife, his babes, and all unfortunate souls
That trace him in his line. No boasting like a fool;
This deed I'll do before this purpose cool.
But no more sights!--Where are these gentlemen?
Come, bring me where they are.

Exeunt

SCENE II.

Fife. Macduff's castle.

Enter LADY MACDUFF, her Son, and ROSS

LADY MACDUFF
What had he done, to make him fly the land?
ROSS
You must have patience, madam.
LADY MACDUFF
He had none:
His flight was madness: when our actions do not,
Our fears do make us traitors.
ROSS
You know not
Whether it was his wisdom or his fear.
LADY MACDUFF
Wisdom! to leave his wife, to leave his babes,
His mansion and his titles in a place
From whence himself does fly? He loves us not;
He wants the natural touch: for the poor wren,
The most diminutive of birds, will fight,
Her young ones in her nest, against the owl.
All is the fear and nothing is the love;
As little is the wisdom, where the flight
So runs against all reason.
ROSS
My dearest coz,
I pray you, school yourself: but for your husband,
He is noble, wise, judicious, and best knows
The fits o' the season. I dare not speak
much further;
But cruel are the times, when we are traitors
And do not know ourselves, when we hold rumour
From what we fear, yet know not what we fear,

But float upon a wild and violent sea
Each way and move. I take my leave of you:
Shall not be long but I'll be here again:
Things at the worst will cease, or else climb upward
To what they were before. My pretty cousin,
Blessing upon you!

LADY MACDUFF
Father'd he is, and yet he's fatherless.

ROSS
I am so much a fool, should I stay longer,
It would be my disgrace and your discomfort:
I take my leave at once.

Exit

LADY MACDUFF
Sirrah, your father's dead;
And what will you do now? How will you live?

Son
As birds do, mother.

LADY MACDUFF
What, with worms and flies?

Son
With what I get, I mean; and so do they.

LADY MACDUFF
Poor bird! thou'ldst never fear the net nor lime,
The pitfall nor the gin.

Son
Why should I, mother? Poor birds they are not set for.
My father is not dead, for all your saying.

LADY MACDUFF
Yes, he is dead; how wilt thou do for a father?

Son
Nay, how will you do for a husband?

LADY MACDUFF

Why, I can buy me twenty at any market.
Son
Then you'll buy 'em to sell again.
LADY MACDUFF
Thou speak'st with all thy wit: and yet, i' faith,
With wit enough for thee.
Son
Was my father a traitor, mother?
LADY MACDUFF
Ay, that he was.
Son
What is a traitor?
LADY MACDUFF
Why, one that swears and lies.
Son
And be all traitors that do so?
LADY MACDUFF
Every one that does so is a traitor, and must be hanged.
Son
And must they all be hanged that swear and lie?
LADY MACDUFF
Every one.
Son
Who must hang them?
LADY MACDUFF
Why, the honest men.
Son
Then the liars and swearers are fools,
for there are liars and swearers enow to beat
the honest men and hang up them.
LADY MACDUFF
Now, God help thee, poor monkey!
But how wilt thou do for a father?
Son

If he were dead, you'ld weep for
him: if you would not, it were a good sign
that I should quickly have a new father.
LADY MACDUFF
Poor prattler, how thou talk'st!

Enter a Messenger

Messenger
Bless you, fair dame! I am not to you known,
Though in your state of honour I am perfect.
I doubt some danger does approach you nearly:
If you will take a homely man's advice,
Be not found here; hence, with your little ones.
To fright you thus, methinks, I am too savage;
To do worse to you were fell cruelty,
Which is too nigh your person. Heaven preserve you!
I dare abide no longer.

Exit

LADY MACDUFF
Whither should I fly?
I have done no harm. But I remember now
I am in this earthly world; where to do harm
Is often laudable, to do good sometime
Accounted dangerous folly: why then, alas,
Do I put up that womanly defence,
To say I have done no harm?

Enter Murderers

What are these faces?
First Murderer
Where is your husband?
LADY MACDUFF

I hope, in no place so unsanctified
Where such as thou mayst find him.
First Murderer
    He's a traitor.
Son
    Thou liest, thou shag-hair'd villain!
First Murderer
    What, you egg!

Stabbing him

    Young fry of treachery!
Son
    He has kill'd me, mother:
    Run away, I pray you!

Dies

Exit LADY MACDUFF, crying 'Murder!' Exeunt Murderers,
following her

SCENE III.

England. Before the King's palace.

Enter MALCOLM and MACDUFF

MALCOLM
    Let us seek out some desolate shade, and there
    Weep our sad bosoms empty.
MACDUFF
    Let us rather
    Hold fast the mortal sword, and like good men
    Bestride our down-fall'n birthdom: each new morn
    New widows howl, new orphans cry, new sorrows
    Strike heaven on the face, that it resounds

As if it felt with Scotland and yell'd out
Like syllable of dolour.
MALCOLM
What I believe I'll wail,
What know believe, and what I can redress,
As I shall find the time to friend, I will.
What you have spoke, it may be so perchance.
This tyrant, whose sole name blisters our tongues,
Was once thought honest: you have loved him well.
He hath not touch'd you yet. I am young;
but something
You may deserve of him through me, and wisdom
To offer up a weak poor innocent lamb
To appease an angry god.
MACDUFF
I am not treacherous.
MALCOLM
But Macbeth is.
A good and virtuous nature may recoil
In an imperial charge. But I shall crave
your pardon;
That which you are my thoughts cannot transpose:
Angels are bright still, though the brightest fell;
Though all things foul would wear the brows of grace,
Yet grace must still look so.
MACDUFF
I have lost my hopes.
MALCOLM
Perchance even there where I did find my doubts.
Why in that rawness left you wife and child,
Those precious motives, those strong knots of love,
Without leave-taking? I pray you,
Let not my jealousies be your dishonours,
But mine own safeties. You may be rightly just,

Whatever I shall think.

MACDUFF

Bleed, bleed, poor country!
Great tyranny! lay thou thy basis sure,
For goodness dare not cheque thee: wear thou
thy wrongs;
The title is affeer'd! Fare thee well, lord:
I would not be the villain that thou think'st
For the whole space that's in the tyrant's grasp,
And the rich East to boot.

MALCOLM

Be not offended:
I speak not as in absolute fear of you.
I think our country sinks beneath the yoke;
It weeps, it bleeds; and each new day a gash
Is added to her wounds: I think withal
There would be hands uplifted in my right;
And here from gracious England have I offer
Of goodly thousands: but, for all this,
When I shall tread upon the tyrant's head,
Or wear it on my sword, yet my poor country
Shall have more vices than it had before,
More suffer and more sundry ways than ever,
By him that shall succeed.

MACDUFF

What should he be?

MALCOLM

It is myself I mean: in whom I know
All the particulars of vice so grafted
That, when they shall be open'd, black Macbeth
Will seem as pure as snow, and the poor state
Esteem him as a lamb, being compared
With my confineless harms.

MACDUFF

Not in the legions
Of horrid hell can come a devil more damn'd
In evils to top Macbeth.

MALCOLM

I grant him bloody,
Luxurious, avaricious, false, deceitful,
Sudden, malicious, smacking of every sin
That has a name: but there's no bottom, none,
In my voluptuousness: your wives, your daughters,
Your matrons and your maids, could not fill up
The cistern of my lust, and my desire
All continent impediments would o'erbear
That did oppose my will: better Macbeth
Than such an one to reign.

MACDUFF

Boundless intemperance
In nature is a tyranny; it hath been
The untimely emptying of the happy throne
And fall of many kings. But fear not yet
To take upon you what is yours: you may
Convey your pleasures in a spacious plenty,
And yet seem cold, the time you may so hoodwink.
We have willing dames enough: there cannot be
That vulture in you, to devour so many
As will to greatness dedicate themselves,
Finding it so inclined.

MALCOLM

With this there grows
In my most ill-composed affection such
A stanchless avarice that, were I king,
I should cut off the nobles for their lands,
Desire his jewels and this other's house:
And my more-having would be as a sauce
To make me hunger more; that I should forge

Quarrels unjust against the good and loyal,
Destroying them for wealth.
MACDUFF
This avarice
Sticks deeper, grows with more pernicious root
Than summer-seeming lust, and it hath been
The sword of our slain kings: yet do not fear;
Scotland hath foisons to fill up your will.
Of your mere own: all these are portable,
With other graces weigh'd.
MALCOLM
But I have none: the king-becoming graces,
As justice, verity, temperance, stableness,
Bounty, perseverance, mercy, lowliness,
Devotion, patience, courage, fortitude,
I have no relish of them, but abound
In the division of each several crime,
Acting it many ways. Nay, had I power, I should
Pour the sweet milk of concord into hell,
Uproar the universal peace, confound
All unity on earth.
MACDUFF
O Scotland, Scotland!
MALCOLM
If such a one be fit to govern, speak:
I am as I have spoken.
MACDUFF
Fit to govern!
No, not to live. O nation miserable,
With an untitled tyrant bloody-scepter'd,
When shalt thou see thy wholesome days again,
Since that the truest issue of thy throne
By his own interdiction stands accursed,
And does blaspheme his breed? Thy royal father

Was a most sainted king: the queen that bore thee,
Oftener upon her knees than on her feet,
Died every day she lived. Fare thee well!
These evils thou repeat'st upon thyself
Have banish'd me from Scotland. O my breast,
Thy hope ends here!
MALCOLM
Macduff, this noble passion,
Child of integrity, hath from my soul
Wiped the black scruples, reconciled my thoughts
To thy good truth and honour. Devilish Macbeth
By many of these trains hath sought to win me
Into his power, and modest wisdom plucks me
From over-credulous haste: but God above
Deal between thee and me! for even now
I put myself to thy direction, and
Unspeak mine own detraction, here abjure
The taints and blames I laid upon myself,
For strangers to my nature. I am yet
Unknown to woman, never was forsworn,
Scarcely have coveted what was mine own,
At no time broke my faith, would not betray
The devil to his fellow and delight
No less in truth than life: my first false speaking
Was this upon myself: what I am truly,
Is thine and my poor country's to command:
Whither indeed, before thy here-approach,
Old Siward, with ten thousand warlike men,
Already at a point, was setting forth.
Now we'll together; and the chance of goodness
Be like our warranted quarrel! Why are you silent?
MACDUFF
Such welcome and unwelcome things at once
'Tis hard to reconcile.

Enter a Doctor

MALCOLM
Well; more anon.--Comes the king forth, I pray you?
Doctor
Ay, sir; there are a crew of wretched souls
That stay his cure: their malady convinces
The great assay of art; but at his touch--
Such sanctity hath heaven given his hand--
They presently amend.
MALCOLM
I thank you, doctor.

Exit Doctor

MACDUFF
What's the disease he means?
MALCOLM
'Tis call'd the evil:
A most miraculous work in this good king;
Which often, since my here-remain in England,
I have seen him do. How he solicits heaven,
Himself best knows: but strangely-visited people,
All swoln and ulcerous, pitiful to the eye,
The mere despair of surgery, he cures,
Hanging a golden stamp about their necks,
Put on with holy prayers: and 'tis spoken,
To the succeeding royalty he leaves
The healing benediction. With this strange virtue,
He hath a heavenly gift of prophecy,
And sundry blessings hang about his throne,
That speak him full of grace.

Enter ROSS

MACDUFF

See, who comes here?

MALCOLM

My countryman; but yet I know him not.

MACDUFF

My ever-gentle cousin, welcome hither.

MALCOLM

I know him now. Good God, betimes remove
The means that makes us strangers!

ROSS

Sir, amen.

MACDUFF

Stands Scotland where it did?

ROSS

Alas, poor country!
Almost afraid to know itself. It cannot
Be call'd our mother, but our grave; where nothing,
But who knows nothing, is once seen to smile;
Where sighs and groans and shrieks that rend the air
Are made, not mark'd; where violent sorrow seems
A modern ecstasy; the dead man's knell
Is there scarce ask'd for who; and good men's lives
Expire before the flowers in their caps,
Dying or ere they sicken.

MACDUFF

O, relation
Too nice, and yet too true!

MALCOLM

What's the newest grief?

ROSS

That of an hour's age doth hiss the speaker:
Each minute teems a new one.

MACDUFF

How does my wife?

ROSS
    Why, well.
MACDUFF
    And all my children?
ROSS
    Well too.
MACDUFF
    The tyrant has not batter'd at their peace?
ROSS
    No; they were well at peace when I did leave 'em.
MACDUFF
    But not a niggard of your speech: how goes't?
ROSS
    When I came hither to transport the tidings,
    Which I have heavily borne, there ran a rumour
    Of many worthy fellows that were out;
    Which was to my belief witness'd the rather,
    For that I saw the tyrant's power a-foot:
    Now is the time of help; your eye in Scotland
    Would create soldiers, make our women fight,
    To doff their dire distresses.
MALCOLM
    Be't their comfort
    We are coming thither: gracious England hath
    Lent us good Siward and ten thousand men;
    An older and a better soldier none
    That Christendom gives out.
ROSS
    Would I could answer
    This comfort with the like! But I have words
    That would be howl'd out in the desert air,
    Where hearing should not latch them.
MACDUFF
    What concern they?

The general cause? or is it a fee-grief
Due to some single breast?

ROSS

No mind that's honest
But in it shares some woe; though the main part
Pertains to you alone.

MACDUFF

If it be mine,
Keep it not from me, quickly let me have it.

ROSS

Let not your ears despise my tongue for ever,
Which shall possess them with the heaviest sound
That ever yet they heard.

MACDUFF

Hum! I guess at it.

ROSS

Your castle is surprised; your wife and babes
Savagely slaughter'd: to relate the manner,
Were, on the quarry of these murder'd deer,
To add the death of you.

MALCOLM

Merciful heaven!
What, man! ne'er pull your hat upon your brows;
Give sorrow words: the grief that does not speak
Whispers the o'er-fraught heart and bids it break.

MACDUFF

My children too?

ROSS

Wife, children, servants, all
That could be found.

MACDUFF

And I must be from thence!
My wife kill'd too?

ROSS

I have said.

MALCOLM

Be comforted:
Let's make us medicines of our great revenge,
To cure this deadly grief.

MACDUFF

He has no children. All my pretty ones?
Did you say all? O hell-kite! All?
What, all my pretty chickens and their dam
At one fell swoop?

MALCOLM

Dispute it like a man.

MACDUFF

I shall do so;
But I must also feel it as a man:
I cannot but remember such things were,
That were most precious to me. Did heaven look on,
And would not take their part? Sinful Macduff,
They were all struck for thee! naught that I am,
Not for their own demerits, but for mine,
Fell slaughter on their souls. Heaven rest them now!

MALCOLM

Be this the whetstone of your sword: let grief
Convert to anger; blunt not the heart, enrage it.

MACDUFF

O, I could play the woman with mine eyes
And braggart with my tongue! But, gentle heavens,
Cut short all intermission; front to front
Bring thou this fiend of Scotland and myself;
Within my sword's length set him; if he 'scape,
Heaven forgive him too!

MALCOLM

This tune goes manly.
Come, go we to the king; our power is ready;

Our lack is nothing but our leave; Macbeth
Is ripe for shaking, and the powers above
Put on their instruments. Receive what cheer you may:
The night is long that never finds the day.

Exeunt

ACT V

SCENE I.

Dunsinane. Ante-room in the castle.

Enter a Doctor of Physic and a Waiting-Gentlewoman

Doctor
    I have two nights watched with you, but can perceive
    no truth in your report. When was it she last walked?
Gentlewoman
    Since his majesty went into the field, I have seen
    her rise from her bed, throw her night-gown upon
    her, unlock her closet, take forth paper, fold it,
    write upon't, read it, afterwards seal it, and again
    return to bed; yet all this while in a most fast sleep.
Doctor
    A great perturbation in nature, to receive at once
    the benefit of sleep, and do the effects of
    watching! In this slumbery agitation, besides her
    walking and other actual performances, what, at any
    time, have you heard her say?
Gentlewoman
    That, sir, which I will not report after her.
Doctor
    You may to me: and 'tis most meet you should.
Gentlewoman
    Neither to you nor any one; having no witness to
    confirm my speech.

Enter LADY MACBETH, with a taper

    Lo you, here she comes! This is her very guise;
    and, upon my life, fast asleep. Observe her; stand close.

Doctor
  How came she by that light?
Gentlewoman
  Why, it stood by her: she has light by her
  continually; 'tis her command.
Doctor
  You see, her eyes are open.
Gentlewoman
  Ay, but their sense is shut.
Doctor
  What is it she does now? Look, how she rubs her hands.
Gentlewoman
  It is an accustomed action with her, to seem thus
  washing her hands: I have known her continue in
  this a quarter of an hour.
LADY MACBETH
  Yet here's a spot.
Doctor
  Hark! she speaks: I will set down what comes from
  her, to satisfy my remembrance the more strongly.
LADY MACBETH
  Out, damned spot! out, I say!--One: two: why,
  then, 'tis time to do't.--Hell is murky!--Fie, my
  lord, fie! a soldier, and afeard? What need we
  fear who knows it, when none can call our power to
  account?--Yet who would have thought the old man
  to have had so much blood in him.
Doctor
  Do you mark that?
LADY MACBETH
  The thane of Fife had a wife: where is she now?--
  What, will these hands ne'er be clean?--No more o'
  that, my lord, no more o' that: you mar all with
  this starting.

Doctor
Go to, go to; you have known what you should not.
Gentlewoman
She has spoke what she should not, I am sure of
that: heaven knows what she has known.
LADY MACBETH
Here's the smell of the blood still: all the
perfumes of Arabia will not sweeten this little
hand. Oh, oh, oh!
Doctor
What a sigh is there! The heart is sorely charged.
Gentlewoman
I would not have such a heart in my bosom for the
dignity of the whole body.
Doctor
Well, well, well,--
Gentlewoman
Pray God it be, sir.
Doctor
This disease is beyond my practise: yet I have known
those which have walked in their sleep who have died
holily in their beds.
LADY MACBETH
Wash your hands, put on your nightgown; look not so
pale.--I tell you yet again, Banquo's buried; he
cannot come out on's grave.
Doctor
Even so?
LADY MACBETH
To bed, to bed! there's knocking at the gate:
come, come, come, come, give me your hand. What's
done cannot be undone.--To bed, to bed, to bed!

Exit

Doctor
　　Will she go now to bed?
Gentlewoman
　　Directly.
Doctor
　　Foul whisperings are abroad: unnatural deeds
　　Do breed unnatural troubles: infected minds
　　To their deaf pillows will discharge their secrets:
　　More needs she the divine than the physician.
　　God, God forgive us all! Look after her;
　　Remove from her the means of all annoyance,
　　And still keep eyes upon her. So, good night:
　　My mind she has mated, and amazed my sight.
　　I think, but dare not speak.
Gentlewoman
　　Good night, good doctor.

Exeunt

SCENE II.

The country near Dunsinane.

*Drum and colours. Enter MENTEITH, CAITHNESS,
ANGUS, LENNOX, and Soldiers*

MENTEITH
　　The English power is near, led on by Malcolm,
　　His uncle Siward and the good Macduff:
　　Revenges burn in them; for their dear causes
　　Would to the bleeding and the grim alarm
　　Excite the mortified man.
ANGUS
　　　　　　　　Near Birnam wood
　　Shall we well meet them; that way are they coming.
CAITHNESS

Who knows if Donalbain be with his brother?
LENNOX
For certain, sir, he is not: I have a file
Of all the gentry: there is Siward's son,
And many unrough youths that even now
Protest their first of manhood.
MENTEITH
What does the tyrant?
CAITHNESS
Great Dunsinane he strongly fortifies:
Some say he's mad; others that lesser hate him
Do call it valiant fury: but, for certain,
He cannot buckle his distemper'd cause
Within the belt of rule.
ANGUS
Now does he feel
His secret murders sticking on his hands;
Now minutely revolts upbraid his faith-breach;
Those he commands move only in command,
Nothing in love: now does he feel his title
Hang loose about him, like a giant's robe
Upon a dwarfish thief.
MENTEITH
Who then shall blame
His pester'd senses to recoil and start,
When all that is within him does condemn
Itself for being there?
CAITHNESS
Well, march we on,
To give obedience where 'tis truly owed:
Meet we the medicine of the sickly weal,
And with him pour we in our country's purge
Each drop of us.
LENNOX

Or so much as it needs,
To dew the sovereign flower and drown the weeds.
Make we our march towards Birnam.

Exeunt, marching

SCENE III.
Dunsinane. A room in the castle.

Enter MACBETH, Doctor, and Attendants

MACBETH
Bring me no more reports; let them fly all:
Till Birnam wood remove to Dunsinane,
I cannot taint with fear. What's the boy Malcolm?
Was he not born of woman? The spirits that know
All mortal consequences have pronounced me thus:
'Fear not, Macbeth; no man that's born of woman
Shall e'er have power upon thee.' Then fly,
false thanes,
And mingle with the English epicures:
The mind I sway by and the heart I bear
Shall never sag with doubt nor shake with fear.

Enter a Servant

The devil damn thee black, thou cream-faced loon!
Where got'st thou that goose look?
Servant
There is ten thousand--
MACBETH
Geese, villain!
Servant
Soldiers, sir.
MACBETH

Go prick thy face, and over-red thy fear,
Thou lily-liver'd boy. What soldiers, patch?
Death of thy soul! those linen cheeks of thine
Are counsellors to fear. What soldiers, whey-face?
Servant
  The English force, so please you.
MACBETH
  Take thy face hence.

Exit Servant

Seyton!--I am sick at heart,
When I behold--Seyton, I say!--This push
Will cheer me ever, or disseat me now.
I have lived long enough: my way of life
Is fall'n into the sear, the yellow leaf;
And that which should accompany old age,
As honour, love, obedience, troops of friends,
I must not look to have; but, in their stead,
Curses, not loud but deep, mouth-honour, breath,
Which the poor heart would fain deny, and dare not.
Seyton!

Enter SEYTON

SEYTON
  What is your gracious pleasure?
MACBETH
  What news more?
SEYTON
  All is confirm'd, my lord, which was reported.
MACBETH
  I'll fight till from my bones my flesh be hack'd.
  Give me my armour.
SEYTON

'Tis not needed yet.

MACBETH
I'll put it on.
Send out more horses; skirr the country round;
Hang those that talk of fear. Give me mine armour.
How does your patient, doctor?

Doctor
Not so sick, my lord,
As she is troubled with thick coming fancies,
That keep her from her rest.

MACBETH
Cure her of that.
Canst thou not minister to a mind diseased,
Pluck from the memory a rooted sorrow,
Raze out the written troubles of the brain
And with some sweet oblivious antidote
Cleanse the stuff'd bosom of that perilous stuff
Which weighs upon the heart?

Doctor
Therein the patient
Must minister to himself.

MACBETH
Throw physic to the dogs; I'll none of it.
Come, put mine armour on; give me my staff.
Seyton, send out. Doctor, the thanes fly from me.
Come, sir, dispatch. If thou couldst, doctor, cast
The water of my land, find her disease,
And purge it to a sound and pristine health,
I would applaud thee to the very echo,
That should applaud again.--Pull't off, I say.--
What rhubarb, cyme, or what purgative drug,
Would scour these English hence? Hear'st thou of them?

Doctor
Ay, my good lord; your royal preparation

Makes us hear something.
MACBETH
　Bring it after me.
　I will not be afraid of death and bane,
　Till Birnam forest come to Dunsinane.
Doctor
　[Aside] Were I from Dunsinane away and clear,
　Profit again should hardly draw me here.

Exeunt

SCENE IV.

Country near Birnam wood.

*Drum and colours. Enter MALCOLM, SIWARD and
YOUNG SIWARD, MACDUFF, MENTEITH, CAITHNESS,
ANGUS, LENNOX, ROSS, and Soldiers, marching*

MALCOLM
　Cousins, I hope the days are near at hand
　That chambers will be safe.
MENTEITH
　We doubt it nothing.
SIWARD
　What wood is this before us?
MENTEITH
　The wood of Birnam.
MALCOLM
　Let every soldier hew him down a bough
　And bear't before him: thereby shall we shadow
　The numbers of our host and make discovery
　Err in report of us.
Soldiers
　It shall be done.
SIWARD

We learn no other but the confident tyrant
Keeps still in Dunsinane, and will endure
Our setting down before 't.

MALCOLM
'Tis his main hope:
For where there is advantage to be given,
Both more and less have given him the revolt,
And none serve with him but constrained things
Whose hearts are absent too.

MACDUFF
Let our just censures
Attend the true event, and put we on
Industrious soldiership.

SIWARD
The time approaches
That will with due decision make us know
What we shall say we have and what we owe.
Thoughts speculative their unsure hopes relate,
But certain issue strokes must arbitrate:
Towards which advance the war.

Exeunt, marching

SCENE V.

Dunsinane. Within the castle.

Enter MACBETH, SEYTON, and Soldiers, with drum and colours

MACBETH
Hang out our banners on the outward walls;
The cry is still 'They come:' our castle's strength
Will laugh a siege to scorn: here let them lie
Till famine and the ague eat them up:
Were they not forced with those that should be ours,

We might have met them dareful, beard to beard,
And beat them backward home.

A cry of women within

What is that noise?
SEYTON
It is the cry of women, my good lord.

Exit

MACBETH
I have almost forgot the taste of fears;
The time has been, my senses would have cool'd
To hear a night-shriek; and my fell of hair
Would at a dismal treatise rouse and stir
As life were in't: I have supp'd full with horrors;
Direness, familiar to my slaughterous thoughts
Cannot once start me.

Re-enter SEYTON

Wherefore was that cry?
SEYTON
The queen, my lord, is dead.
MACBETH
She should have died hereafter;
There would have been a time for such a word.
To-morrow, and to-morrow, and to-morrow,
Creeps in this petty pace from day to day
To the last syllable of recorded time,
And all our yesterdays have lighted fools
The way to dusty death. Out, out, brief candle!
Life's but a walking shadow, a poor player
That struts and frets his hour upon the stage
And then is heard no more: it is a tale

Told by an idiot, full of sound and fury,
Signifying nothing.

Enter a Messenger

Thou comest to use thy tongue; thy story quickly.
Messenger
Gracious my lord,
I should report that which I say I saw,
But know not how to do it.
MACBETH
Well, say, sir.
Messenger
As I did stand my watch upon the hill,
I look'd toward Birnam, and anon, methought,
The wood began to move.
MACBETH
Liar and slave!
Messenger
Let me endure your wrath, if't be not so:
Within this three mile may you see it coming;
I say, a moving grove.
MACBETH
If thou speak'st false,
Upon the next tree shalt thou hang alive,
Till famine cling thee: if thy speech be sooth,
I care not if thou dost for me as much.
I pull in resolution, and begin
To doubt the equivocation of the fiend
That lies like truth: 'Fear not, till Birnam wood
Do come to Dunsinane:' and now a wood
Comes toward Dunsinane. Arm, arm, and out!
If this which he avouches does appear,
There is nor flying hence nor tarrying here.
I gin to be aweary of the sun,

And wish the estate o' the world were now undone.
Ring the alarum-bell! Blow, wind! come, wrack!
At least we'll die with harness on our back.

Exeunt

SCENE VI.

Dunsinane. Before the castle.

Drum and colours. Enter MALCOLM, SIWARD,
MACDUFF, and their Army, with boughs

MALCOLM
Now near enough: your leafy screens throw down.
And show like those you are. You, worthy uncle,
Shall, with my cousin, your right-noble son,
Lead our first battle: worthy Macduff and we
Shall take upon 's what else remains to do,
According to our order.
SIWARD
Fare you well.
Do we but find the tyrant's power to-night,
Let us be beaten, if we cannot fight.
MACDUFF
Make all our trumpets speak; give them all breath,
Those clamorous harbingers of blood and death.

Exeunt

SCENE VII.

Another part of the field.

Alarums. Enter MACBETH

MACBETH
They have tied me to a stake; I cannot fly,

105

But, bear-like, I must fight the course. What's he
That was not born of woman? Such a one
Am I to fear, or none.

Enter YOUNG SIWARD

YOUNG SIWARD
What is thy name?
MACBETH
Thou'lt be afraid to hear it.
YOUNG SIWARD
No; though thou call'st thyself a hotter name
Than any is in hell.
MACBETH
My name's Macbeth.
YOUNG SIWARD
The devil himself could not pronounce a title
More hateful to mine ear.
MACBETH
No, nor more fearful.
YOUNG SIWARD
Thou liest, abhorred tyrant; with my sword
I'll prove the lie thou speak'st.

They fight and YOUNG SIWARD is slain

MACBETH
Thou wast born of woman
But swords I smile at, weapons laugh to scorn,
Brandish'd by man that's of a woman born.

Exit

Alarums. Enter MACDUFF

MACDUFF

That way the noise is. Tyrant, show thy face!
If thou be'st slain and with no stroke of mine,
My wife and children's ghosts will haunt me still.
I cannot strike at wretched kerns, whose arms
Are hired to bear their staves: either thou, Macbeth,
Or else my sword with an unbatter'd edge
I sheathe again undeeded. There thou shouldst be;
By this great clatter, one of greatest note
Seems bruited. Let me find him, fortune!
And more I beg not.

Exit. Alarums

Enter MALCOLM and SIWARD

SIWARD
This way, my lord; the castle's gently render'd:
The tyrant's people on both sides do fight;
The noble thanes do bravely in the war;
The day almost itself professes yours,
And little is to do.
MALCOLM
We have met with foes
That strike beside us.
SIWARD
Enter, sir, the castle.

Exeunt. Alarums

SCENE VIII.

Another part of the field.

Enter MACBETH

MACBETH
Why should I play the Roman fool, and die
On mine own sword? whiles I see lives, the gashes
Do better upon them.

Enter MACDUFF

MACDUFF
Turn, hell-hound, turn!
MACBETH
Of all men else I have avoided thee:
But get thee back; my soul is too much charged
With blood of thine already.
MACDUFF
I have no words:
My voice is in my sword: thou bloodier villain
Than terms can give thee out!

They fight

MACBETH
Thou losest labour:
As easy mayst thou the intrenchant air
With thy keen sword impress as make me bleed:
Let fall thy blade on vulnerable crests;
I bear a charmed life, which must not yield,
To one of woman born.
MACDUFF
Despair thy charm;
And let the angel whom thou still hast served
Tell thee, Macduff was from his mother's womb

Untimely ripp'd.

MACBETH

Accursed be that tongue that tells me so,
For it hath cow'd my better part of man!
And be these juggling fiends no more believed,
That palter with us in a double sense;
That keep the word of promise to our ear,
And break it to our hope. I'll not fight with thee.

MACDUFF

Then yield thee, coward,
And live to be the show and gaze o' the time:
We'll have thee, as our rarer monsters are,
Painted on a pole, and underwrit,
'Here may you see the tyrant.'

MACBETH

I will not yield,
To kiss the ground before young Malcolm's feet,
And to be baited with the rabble's curse.
Though Birnam wood be come to Dunsinane,
And thou opposed, being of no woman born,
Yet I will try the last. Before my body
I throw my warlike shield. Lay on, Macduff,
And damn'd be him that first cries, 'Hold, enough!'

Exeunt, fighting. Alarums

Retreat. Flourish. Enter, with drum and colours,
MALCOLM, SIWARD, ROSS, the other Thanes, and Soldiers

MALCOLM

I would the friends we miss were safe arrived.

SIWARD

Some must go off: and yet, by these I see,
So great a day as this is cheaply bought.

MALCOLM
  Macduff is missing, and your noble son.
ROSS
  Your son, my lord, has paid a soldier's debt:
  He only lived but till he was a man;
  The which no sooner had his prowess confirm'd
  In the unshrinking station where he fought,
  But like a man he died.
SIWARD
  Then he is dead?
ROSS
  Ay, and brought off the field: your cause of sorrow
  Must not be measured by his worth, for then
  It hath no end.
SIWARD
  Had he his hurts before?
ROSS
  Ay, on the front.
SIWARD
  Why then, God's soldier be he!
  Had I as many sons as I have hairs,
  I would not wish them to a fairer death:
  And so, his knell is knoll'd.
MALCOLM
  He's worth more sorrow,
  And that I'll spend for him.
SIWARD
  He's worth no more
  They say he parted well, and paid his score:
  And so, God be with him! Here comes newer comfort.
Re-enter MACDUFF, with MACBETH's head

MACDUFF
  Hail, king! for so thou art: behold, where stands

The usurper's cursed head: the time is free:
I see thee compass'd with thy kingdom's pearl,
That speak my salutation in their minds;
Whose voices I desire aloud with mine:
Hail, King of Scotland!
ALL
Hail, King of Scotland!

Flourish

MALCOLM
We shall not spend a large expense of time
Before we reckon with your several loves,
And make us even with you. My thanes and kinsmen,
Henceforth be earls, the first that ever Scotland
In such an honour named. What's more to do,
Which would be planted newly with the time,
As calling home our exiled friends abroad
That fled the snares of watchful tyranny;
Producing forth the cruel ministers
Of this dead butcher and his fiend-like queen,
Who, as 'tis thought, by self and violent hands
Took off her life; this, and what needful else
That calls upon us, by the grace of Grace,
We will perform in measure, time and place:
So, thanks to all at once and to each one,
Whom we invite to see us crown'd at Scone.

Flourish. Exeunt

Biography

A Short Life of Edward de Vere, 17th Earl of Oxford

by Dr. Kevin Gilvary, President
The de Vere Society

He was born on 12 April 1550 at Castle Hedingham, his family's ancestral home. His father, John de Vere, 16th Earl, was Lord Great Chamberlain and attended the coronations of both Mary and Elizabeth Tudor. His mother was Margaret Golding. Edward was 11 when, in 1561, Queen Elizabeth visited Hedingham for four days of masques, feasting and entertainments. When his father died in 1562, young Oxford left to become, like Bertram in *All's Well that Ends Well*, a ward of the Crown under the guardianship of William Cecil, the Queen's private secretary (later Lord Burghley, Lord Treasurer). His mother married Charles Tyrrell and seems to have passed out of the boy's life. His sister Mary went to live with her stepfather and the siblings were not reunited for some years.

According to a curriculum in Cecil's own hand, Edward de Vere's daily studies included dancing, French, Latin, writing and drawing, cosmography, penmanship, riding, shooting, exercise and prayer. Edward de Vere showed a prodigious talent for scholarship from his early years, and we may ascribe his lifelong love of learning to the influence of two of his early tutors. The first was Sir Thomas Smith who was, perhaps, England's most respected Greek scholar and the former Cambridge tutor of Sir William Cecil. It was, no doubt, through Cecil's influence that Edward de Vere spent some time living in the household of Smith in his early years, during which time he spent about five months at Smith's alma mater, Queens' College, Cambridge. Smith was a scholar of widely varied interests – this was reflected in his 400-volume library, some of which is still extant at Cambridge. De Vere's other tutor was Laurence Nowell, who was not only an accomplished cartographer but was also England's premier scholar of Anglo-Saxon literature – it was Nowell who possessed the only known copy of *Beowulf.*

Another important influence on Edward de Vere's early studies was his maternal uncle Arthur Golding, an officer in the Court of Wards under Cecil, who is credited with the translation of Ovid's *Metamorphoses*, published in 1567, a book widely recognised as having a major influence on 'Shakespeare'.

Following on from his matriculation at Cambridge in November 1558, Edward was awarded an honorary MA by Cambridge during a Royal progress in August 1564, and another degree by Oxford University during a Royal progress in 1566. Edward de Vere then attended Gray's Inn to study law. One notable feature of the Elizabethan Inns of Court was a tradition of mounting dramatic productions and of hosting the various touring companies of players.

In 1570 he served in a military campaign in Scotland under the Earl of Sussex. By 1571, he was reported as a leading luminary of the Court and, for a time, a favourite of Queen Elizabeth. In December 1571 he married Anne Cecil, aged 15, daughter of his guardian. This was a dynastic marriage where all the advantage accrued to Cecil who, ennobled as Baron Burghley, had reduced the social gap between himself and the young Earl.

While Oxford was away on a Grand Tour of Europe, he heard that his daughter Elizabeth Vere had been born in July 1575. On his return in early 1576, he appeared to have been convinced that Elizabeth was not his child; consequently he became estranged from Anne for five years, and exiled himself from Court, taking up residence in the Savoy and concerning himself with literary and musical patronage.

Already, in 1573, *Cardanus Comfort* (the Consolations of Boethius) had been translated from Latin by Thomas Bedingfield and dedicated to Oxford; and published with a preface written by him. In 1576 an anthology, *A Paradise of Daintie Devices*, including several poems by Oxford, was published. These are juvenile works but already show affinities, in both style and thought, with those of the mature Shakespeare.

Oxford's Grand Tour had taken in Paris, Strasbourg, Venice, Genoa, Florence, Palermo and, on his way back through France, Rousillon – the setting for *Love's Labour's Lost*. Oxford spent the best part of a year travelling in Italy in 1576, and becoming involved with moneylenders. He came back to England fluent in Italian and well acquainted with the northern Italian cities, to be satirised by Gabriel Harvey as 'The Italian Earl'. On his way back his ship was attacked by pirates in the English Channel (cf. *Hamlet*). Fourteen of 'Shakespeare's' plays have Italian settings, in which he put his detailed knowledge of the country, beyond pure book knowledge, to good use.

1573 saw the birth of Henry Wriothesley, Earl of Southampton. Although history has not bequeathed to us any evidence of a direct relationship between the two men, in the relatively small world of the royal Court, they must have been acquainted with each other. The poems *Venus and Adonis* (1593) and *The Rape of Lucrece* (1594)

were dedicated to Southampton. These were the first
works to be published under the name 'Shakespeare' and
for the next five years the records show the byline
'Shakespeare' to have been associated exclusively with
these two poems. Plays under the name 'Shakespeare' did
not appear in print until 1598, the year that Lord
Burghley died.

In May 1577 Oxford invested in Frobisher's
voyage in the ship *Edward Bonaventure*. Despite its
name, the ship's voyage across the Atlantic in search of
the North-West Passage lost money; consequently he was
forced to sell three estates (cf. Hamlet's words 'I am but
mad north-north-west' II.1.). In 1578 he invested in
Frobisher's second expedition, which also lost money,
forcing further sales of estates.

He was mentioned by Gabriel Harvey in an
address to Queen Elizabeth in July 1578, as a prolific
private poet and one 'whose countenance shakes spears'.
In the same year John Lyly, Oxford's secretary, published
Euphues.The Anatomy of Wit, followed in 1579 by
Euphues and his England, dedicated to Oxford. These
two books launched the fashion for 'Euphuism', a style
characterized by high-flown language, satirized in *Love's
Labour's Lost*.

In March 1581 Oxford's mistress, Anne Vavasour,
who was one of Queen Elizabeth's Ladies of the
Bedchamber, gave birth to a son. The lovers and their son
were sent to the Tower by an infuriated Queen but swiftly
released (cf. *Measure for Measure*). After his release,
Oxford was wounded in a street-fight provoked by
Thomas Knyvet, a kinsman of Anne Vavasour; affrays
continued in the streets of London between the rival
gangs of supporters for over a year (cf.*Romeo and Juliet*).

In December 1581 he resumed living with his
long-suffering and devoted wife, and accepted Elizabeth

Vere as his child. Tragically, their only son died one day after his birth. Three more daughters followed, of whom Susan and Bridget survived.

In 1584, Robert Greene's *Gwydonius; the Card of Fancy* was dedicated to him, identifying him as a 'pre-eminent writer'. In 1586, when he was 36, he served on the tribunal which condemned Mary, Queen of Scots to execution.

In the same year, the Queen awarded Oxford an unconditional pension of £1,000 a year for life (about £500,000 at today's value). The motive for this uncharacteristic generosity on the part of the Queen remains a mystery – no accounting was required of Oxford. Her successor, King James I, continued to pay the pension. In reply to Sir Robert Cecil's request that Lord Sheffield's pension be increased, the King refused, saying, 'Great Oxford got no more . . .', leaving us to wonder why Great Oxford? His greatness does not seem to have resided in war or any of the known offices of State. Perhaps a clue can be found in a letter to Burghley, written in 1594, in which Edward de Vere seeks his favour in a matter involving what he describes as 'in mine office' and that this office is beholden to the Queen.

In 1589, George Puttenham published *The Arte of English Poesie* and this contains the most telling recognition of Edward de Vere's literary standing amongst his contemporaries: 'And in her Majesties time that now is are sprong up an other crew of Courtly makers Noble men and Gentlemen of her Majesties owne servantes, who have written excellently well as it would appear if their doings could be found out and made publicke with the rest, of which number is first that noble Gentleman Edward Earle of Oxford.'

In 1588 his wife Anne, daughter of Lord Burghley, died and in extant letters written at this time, it is reported

116

that Burghley is so incapacitated by grief over the death of his favourite daughter that he is incapable of conducting any Privy Council business.

Three years later, in 1591, Oxford married another of the Queen's Maids of Honour, Elizabeth Trentham, with whom he finally became the father of a male heir; Henry de Vere, 18th Earl of Oxford. Although there is evidence of his continued involvement in Court affairs, from the date of this marriage Edward de Vere's life at his new home at King's Place in Hackney is perhaps the most obscure of his entire life.

In 1594, his ship the *Edward Bonaventure* was wrecked in Bermuda (cf. *The Tempest*). In January 1595, Elizabeth Vere married William Stanley, 6th Earl of Derby, another literary earl who maintained his own company of players – many scholars believe that *A Midsummer Night's Dream* was written for these festivities which were attended by the whole royal Court.

On September 7 1598, Francis Meres' *Palladis Tamia* was registered for publication, naming Oxford as the 'best for comedy'. This is a vital document in Shakespearean history because it includes the first mention of 'Shakespeare' as a playwright, attributing twelve plays to him; until then Shakespeare's reputation had rested on the two narrative poems only.

Oxford suffered all his life from financial difficulties, much of which can be traced to the fact that Queen Elizabeth handed out the bulk of his estate to her favourite courtier the Earl of Leicester during Oxford's minority as a royal ward (estates which Oxford found almost impossible to reclaim), and the ruinous debt she placed upon him over his marriage to Anne Cecil. It is, however, notable that his new brother-in-law, the wealthy Staffordshire landowner and Knight of the Shire Francis Trentham, took over the management of Edward de

117

Vere's near-bankrupt estate from 1591 and gradually nursed it back to health so that, when Oxford died, all of his massive debts had been cleared.

On the Queen's death in 1603 Oxford wrote eloquently to Sir Robert Cecil, son and heir of Lord Burghley, of his 'great grief'. He wrote, 'In this common shipwreck, mine is above all the rest, who least regarded, though often comforted, she hath left to try my fortune among the alterations of time and chance'.

Oxford died in Hackney in 1604, cause unknown. Parish records state that he was buried in Hackney Church on July 6, but a family history by his first cousin Percival Golding, states 'Edward de Veer ... a man in mind and body absolutely accomplished with honorable endowments ... lieth buried at Westminster'. No record of such a burial can now be traced in Westminster Abbey, where there is a Vere family tomb.

The Aftermath of Oxford's life and death

During the winter season 1604-05, six of Shakespeare's plays were presented at Court by command of King James I. This has an air of commemoration. In 1609 the *Sonnets* were published in a pirated edition. The famous dedication describes the author as 'our ever-living', a phrase invariably used only of the dead.

In 1622 Henry Peacham published, in *The Compleat Gentelman*, a list of poets who made Elizabeth's reign a 'golden age'. Unaccountably, he omitted Shakespeare but placed the Earl of Oxford in first place in his list – perhaps he knew them to be the same person. This is unlike Meres who included them both – maybe one reason was because he didn't know Oxford and Shakespeare were the same person.

We do not know who instigated publication of the First Folio Edition of the Shakespeare plays in 1623, but there is no mention of any executor or relative of Shakspere of Stratford in connection with it. However, of the two brothers who financed it and to whom it was dedicated, one – Philip Earl of Montgomery – was the husband of Oxford's daughter Susan, while the other – William Earl of Pembroke – had once been a suitor for her sister Bridget. Pembroke was Lord Chamberlain, the supreme authority in the world of theatre, and thus in a position to decide which plays were to be published and which suppressed. We also know that Ben Jonson, who wrote much of the introductory material, was an intimate associate of the de Vere family after Oxford's death. The First Folio was therefore very much a family affair, but the family was not the one in Stratford-on-Avon.

An AfterVerse

For those with yet an interest
In strenuous debate
We've compiled a list of books and films
Your appetite to sate.
From this study clear your mind
Of doubt and all misgiving-
Who from us has long since gone
And who is ever-living.

Selected References & Bibliography
About the Author
Edward de Vere, 17th Earl of Oxford

Books

♦ Anderson, M. (2005). *Shakespeare by Another Name: The Life of Edward de Vere, Earl of Oxford, The Man who was Shakespeare.* New York: Gotham Books. *--A physicist by training with research interest in how evidence supports or negates a theory, Mark Anderson spent ten years investigating Edward de Vere as the author of Shake-speare's works.*

♦Farina, William. (2006). *De Vere as Shakespeare: An Oxfordian Reading of the Canon.* Jefferson, NC. McFarland & Company.

--Each of the plays and poems is individually assessed and explored in its own chapter, using the innumerable connections between the text itself and the life of its author, Edward de Vere.

♦ Looney, J. Thomas (2018). *Shakespeare Identified.* Cary, N.C. Veritas Publicaations.
--First published in 1920 this book began the modern Oxfordian movement. From reading it, Sigmund Freud became convinced and John Galsworthy called it "the best detective story I ever read."

♦ Ogburn, C. (1992). *The Mysterious William Shakespeare.* McLean (Va.): EPM.
--An in depth exploration and must read foundational book on the authorship question.

♦Sobran, Joseph. (1997). *Alias Shakespeare: Solving the Greatest Literary Mystery of All Time.*
New York; The Free Press, A Division of Simon & Schuster.
--A concise exploration of the puzzling questions surrounding the authorship controversy with the evidence decisively supporting the case for Edward de Vere, the 17th Earl of Oxford, as the rightful author of the Shakespeare plays and poems.

♦Whittemore, Hank. (2016), *100 Reasons Shake-speare Was the Earl of Oxford.*
Somerville MA. Forever Press.
►Also with further discussion and public comment at: *Hank Whittemore's Shakespeare Blog.*
        https://hankwhittemore.com/
--In both the book and online blog cited above, Whittemore presents a concise introduction to the

authorship question that examines 100 different aspects, from biographical and historical records, that point to Edward de Vere as the true writer of the Shake-speare plays and poems.

Websites & Videos

▶ De Vere Society. (2019). The de Vere Society – Dedicated to the proposition that the works of Shakespeare were written by Edward de Vere, 17th Earl of Oxford. [online] Deveresociety.co.uk. Available at: https://deveresociety.co.uk
--A very complete resource with substantial biographical and authorship information and links.

▶ The Oxford Fellowship (2019). Shakespeare Oxford Fellowship | Research and Discussion of the Shakespeare Authorship Question. [online] Shakespeare Oxford Fellowship. Available at: https://shakespeareoxfordfellowship.org/
--A seminal online resource especially focusing on the authorship question.

▶ Waugh, A. (2019). Alexander Waugh. [online] YouTube. Available at: https://www.youtube.com/channel/UCHN7SCKlsa9lPYJ mqqQ2uIg/featured/
OR simply search: 'Alexander Waugh'
--Alexander Waugh is a leading authorship scholar who has produced many fascinating video presentations on the authorship question. This link is to his YouTube Channel.

▶ Columbia Pictures & Centropolis Entertainment. (2011). *Anonymous.* Produced and directed by Roland Emmerich. [DVD]
--This mainstream film is both entertaining and enlightening. It presents a superb dramatization of the character of Edward de Vere, setting out in detail the historical and personal context which made his anonymous authorship necessary.

▶Centropolis Entertainment and First Folio Pictures. *Last Will and Testament.* (2012). [DVD]
--A thoughtful and ground-breaking video documentary introduction to the Shakespeare authorship question.

Acknowledgment
Our sincere thanks to
The de Vere Society
and
The Shakespeare Oxford Fellowship
*for their inspiration, help and support
in creating this series.*

Attributions
*--Character list from Wikipedia under
the Creative Commons License 3.0
--Play text from the Moby(tm) editions
in the public domain*

Photos
Coat of Arms of Edward de Vere
Source: Wikimedia.org
Author: George Baker / Public domain

The Keep at Castle Hedingham
Source: geograph.org.uk
Author: David Phillips / CC BY-SA 2.0

The de Vere Family Coat of Arms
Source: Wikimedia
Author: Rs-nourse / CC BY-SA 3.0
(https://creativecommons.org/licenses/by-sa/3.0)

View from The Minstrels' Gallery, Hedingham Castle
Source: geograph.org.uk/p/3162585
Photo by: © PAUL FARMER - cc-by-sa/2.0

Cover/Inside: The Welbeck portrait of Edward de Vere (1575).
Artist unknown. National Portrait Gallery, London.

This work has been edited and produced by

Verus Publishing
www.verusbooks.com

V | P